Violence Against Women

Look for these and other books in the Lucent Overview Series:

Advertising
Alcoholism
Censorship
Child Abuse
Children's Rights
Civil Rights
Depression
Drug Abuse
Family Violence
Gun Control
Homeless Children
Homelessness
Juvenile Crime
Police Brutality
Poverty
Prisons
Sexual Harassment
Women's Rights

Violence Against Women

by Lisa Wolff

LUCENT BOOKS

LUCENT Overview Series

LUCENT Overview Series

Library of Congress Cataloging-in-Publication Data

Wolff, Lisa, 1954–
Violence against women / Lisa Wolff.
p. cm. — (Lucent overview series)
Includes bibliographical references and index.
Summary: Discusses violence against women including domestic violence and rape, as well as the American culture of sex and violence, getting help for victims, and ideas for prevention.
ISBN 1-56006-509-5 (alk. paper)
1. Women—Crimes against—United States—Juvenile literature. 2. Wife abuse—United States—Juvenile literature. 3. Rape—United States—Juvenile literature. 4. Abused women—United States—Juvenile literature. [1. Women—Crimes against. 2. Wife abuse. 3. Rape. 4. Abused women. 5. Violence.] I. Title. II. Series.
HV6250.4.W65W65 1999
362.83'0973—dc21

98-7614
CIP
AC

P.O. Box 289011, San Diego, CA 92198-9011
Printed in the U.S.A.

Contents

Introduction

FBI STATISTICS SHOW that a woman is beaten by a man every twelve seconds in the United States. Its studies estimate that one in two women will be assaulted by a male partner during her lifetime, and every six hours a woman is killed in an act of domestic violence.

Unless a woman dies at the hands of her abuser, it is likely that her abuse will go unreported. This is especially true when the abuser is her husband or boyfriend. Most physical abuse takes place behind closed doors, and fear and shame often keep battered women silent.

While statistics vary, there is no question that violence against women is a serious and widespread problem with a long history. Its roots are buried deep in a culture that for hundreds of years considered women inferior to men—and even as their property. Though equality of the sexes is now written into American law, the attitudes that kept men in power for centuries do not die easily, nor does the belief among many men that they have a right to express that power through physical force.

Violence against women: a complex problem

Violence against women takes many forms. It is most often committed by a husband or partner, but some of the most brutal attacks are by strangers. Battering, stalking, sexual assault, and rape occur in all parts of the country every day. Men who abuse women cross all lines of class, race, and religion. What they all have in common is a need to control and a feeling that their only way to maintain power is through the threat of physical force.

The reasons men commit violent acts against women are complex. Beating, rape, and death threats are more than just symptoms of a society that promotes male power. Most men do not abuse women, and those who do have serious problems with anger and self-esteem. Many batterers were themselves abused as children and learned to express uncomfortable feelings the way their fathers did—through violent acts.

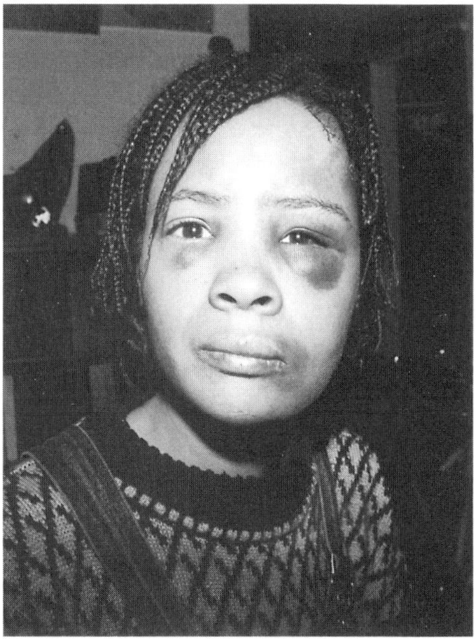

Bruised and swollen, a battered woman's face attests to the habitual abuse to which she is subjected.

For many years abused women were blamed for letting themselves be victims. The police and the courts were reluctant to get involved in domestic violence cases, considering them private problems for families to work out on their own. They pointed to all the women who ended up dropping charges against their abusers as a waste of the justice system's time. Even victims of rape were commonly blamed for provoking the crime, and details of their personal lives were dragged into court to prove they had "asked for it."

Because of the way they could expect to be treated by authorities, victims of male violence felt there was nowhere to turn for help. Those who escaped abusive relationships often returned to their abusers. Many rape victims failed to report their attacks, knowing their chances of victory in court were slim and that their lives could be ruined in the process.

Change comes slowly

Over the past two decades, attitudes and laws have been changing to recognize and protect women's rights. The women's movement of the 1970s started this process, as women began to demand that batterers be arrested and that abused women be helped. They pushed for changes in the law and started shelters and counseling for women in danger. Laws that protect rape victims from unfair treatment in court and laws against stalking—following or threatening victims—are recent results of women's lobbying for equal rights.

Society, however, is slower to change than the law. Many men continue to abuse women because they know they can often get away with it. The criminal justice system has improved in its dealing with male violence, but many police officers and judges remain slow in providing protection for women. Programs for battered women and victims of rape are underfunded, and little attention has been paid to helping abusive men change. Even when rapists and murderers are jailed, they receive little treatment and often repeat their crimes once they are freed.

The media, too, often portrays women being dominated by men. Movies, television, and advertisements are filled with women shown as sex objects, whose only apparent value is in providing pleasure for men. They are often portrayed as male fantasy figures, young, beautiful, and weak, who easily fall under the power of men; or, they may be "bad" women, who seduce men and deserve to be punished. Sex and violence are blended on the screen in a way that makes brutal crimes like rape look glamorous.

Although change has been slow, there has been some progress. More women are reporting the crimes committed against them, and more men are being convicted and getting help. As women gain economic power, they are in a better position to walk away from abusive partners. Their protests against images that are insulting to women are being heard, and portrayals of strong, capable women are becoming more common. American society is gradually coming to understand the nature of violence against women and to treat it as a serious crime.

1

Domestic Violence and the Law

DOMESTIC VIOLENCE IS any violent or threatening behavior between family members, including former husbands and wives. The term is now also applied to abusive acts between unmarried partners who live together. The National Coalition Against Domestic Violence defines it as "a pattern of behavior with the effect of establishing power and control over another person through fear and intimidation."[1]

Researchers estimate that domestic violence occurs every fourteen seconds in the United States. Studies show that over 2 million women are severely beaten in their homes each year and that half of all couples have had at least one violent incident. Domestic violence is the leading cause of injury to women in the United States. According to the U.S. attorney general's office, 94 percent of violence between partners involves a man beating a woman.

Domestic violence has a long history throughout the world. Based on the ancient belief that men are superior to women, it was supported for thousands of years by economic, social, and religious institutions. Though most societies offered some legal protection for women, these laws usually applied to only the worst cases of abuse.

Early law

In past centuries wives were considered the property of their husbands and could be physically forced to obey their orders. The fifteenth-century Rules of Marriage in Sienna,

Italy, provide a telling picture of attitudes at the time: "When you see your wife commit an offense, don't rush at her with insults and violent blows, rather, first correct her lovingly. [If this fails] scold her sharply, bully, and terrify her. And if this still doesn't work . . . take up a stick and beat her soundly."[2]

Both England and the United States had laws against wife beating by the eighteenth century, though they were not well enforced. In nineteenth-century America, men were allowed to use "reasonable chastisement" to get their wives to behave. Since women were still considered the property of their husbands, it was a man's duty to keep his wife in line. An 1864 ruling in North Carolina states that "the law permits him to use toward his wife such a degree of force as is necessary to control an unruly temper and make her behave herself; and unless some permanent injury be afflicted, or there be an excess of violence . . . the law will not invade the domestic forum, or go behind the curtain."[3]

It was not until 1871, in an Alabama court decision, that a husband was denied the right to physically punish his wife even "moderately." And it took another century for laws against domestic violence to be seriously enforced.

The feminist movement

Violence in the home remained largely hidden until the 1970s, when women began to join forces to demand their rights. The few women who dared to speak out about their abuse were blamed for provoking the violence and shamed into silence.

The feminist movement began in the 1960s, but it took a decade before real progress was made. Women working in local communities established over one thousand shelters throughout the United States and at least one thousand domestic abuse hot lines. They pressured states to enact domestic abuse prevention laws and demanded enforcement. Groups of battered women brought class-action suits against police departments and court officers who failed to arrest and prosecute abusers.

The feminist movement dramatically changed society's perception of domestic violence during the 1970s. Members of the organization Women Against Pornography protest violence against women in 1979.

Under the pressure of the women's groups, many states adopted domestic violence prevention acts, which gave police departments and the courts more authority to take action. Domestic violence began to be viewed as a crime, and cases were moved from civil to criminal courts. This was an important step since civil court judges are not given the assailant's criminal records. Therefore, judges sometimes freed men with outstanding criminal warrants, who returned home to beat—or even kill—their partners.

Feminists also set out to educate people about the problem of domestic violence. In addition to starting support and education groups for the battered women themselves, they set up education and training programs for police officers, prosecutors, and judges to teach them how to deal with domestic abuse. They also established programs to help men understand and stop their abuse, recognizing that simply throwing husbands and fathers in jail was not a good solution. Domestic violence awareness programs were started in schools, and women worked with hospitals and child protective services to help the children battered women could not protect.

Despite all these efforts, progress was slow and unsteady. Even today, some states do not try domestic assault cases in criminal court, and changing laws does not always change attitudes and behavior. Still, the women's movement succeeded in making major changes in American society. It encouraged women to speak out against their abuse and gave them places to turn for shelter, support, and legal aid.

Court cases that helped change the law

The legal protections women won in the 1970s were tested during the next decade. In 1984, Tracy Thurman won a landmark lawsuit in federal district court against the city of Torrington, Connecticut, and twenty-six police officers. The defendants were charged with violating Thurman's constitutional rights of equal protection under the Fourteenth Amendment.

Thurman had left her battering husband, Charles, in 1982. When he continued to harass her and threatened to kill her and her son, she got a court order of protection against him. Police officers ignored the court order and failed to respond quickly when her husband showed up to assault her. Thurman's husband beat and stabbed her, and police did not restrain him until she was disfigured and partially paralyzed.

The Fourteenth Amendment to the U.S. Constitution had previously been used only in cases of race discrimination. According to a legal scholar, "Just as racial prejudice stopped police from enforcing the laws and arresting offenders, so contemporary sexist attitudes underlie the police's failure to respond to battered women's pleas for help."[4]

Thurman was awarded $2.3 million in damages in 1985. As a result of this ruling, Connecticut adopted a new domestic violence law requiring the arrest of people who assault their spouses. In the twelve months after the law took effect, the number of arrests for domestic violence in the state jumped 93 percent. Connecticut was not the first state to adopt a mandatory arrest law—Oregon had one as early as 1979—but the publicity surrounding the Thurman case convinced other states to follow suit.

Women across the country were encouraged by Thurman's victory, but there were many setbacks. Perhaps the most damaging occurred in 1989, in the decision of *DeShaney v. Winnebago*. In this case, Melody DeShaney sued the Winnebago County Department of Social Services for failing to stop the beatings her former husband, Randy DeShaney, inflicted on their four-year-old son, Joshua. The boy was beaten into a coma in 1984 and placed in an institution for life. Melody DeShaney charged that the department had "deprived Joshua of his liberty without due process of law, in violation of his rights under the Fourteenth Amendment, by failing to intervene to protect him against a risk of violence at his father's hands of which they knew or should have known."[5] The lower courts ruled against her, but the U.S. Supreme

Reprinted by permission of Kirk Anderson.

Court heard her appeal. It used this case to define when a government agency's failure to protect an individual is a violation of that person's due process rights. The Court's decision against DeShaney was based on its opinion that due process was "to protect people from the State, not to ensure that the State protected them from each other."[6]

This decision had a serious negative effect on future domestic violence cases. It lowered the responsibility of government agencies, including the police, to protect women and children from abuse by men. Prosecuting attorneys had to find other ways of winning their cases against abusers, such as building stronger equal protection suits or suing cities for failing to train their police departments to handle domestic violence calls correctly.

Women's groups have brought about many changes in the law over the past two decades to protect the rights and safety of abused women. They have also worked hard to see that these laws get enforced. One of the first steps women can take to protect themselves against a violent or threatening partner is getting an order of protection.

Court orders of protection

Orders of protection, sometimes also called no-contact orders, emergency orders of protection, or temporary restraining orders, are issued in court before a judge. They prohibit the abuser from physical violence, harassment, stalking, or threatening his partner with bodily harm or rape. The details of court orders vary from state to state.

To get an order of protection, a woman needs a police report of an abusive incident. The state provides her with an attorney, and the abuser is served with a summons or warrant by a judge in court, in the victim's presence. The court order lasts for a period of time established by the state, until the state proves its case against the abuser. It can be extended by appearing in court at an appointed date and time. The accused is provided with an attorney if he cannot afford to hire his own.

In addition to keeping the abuser out of his victim's home, the court has the power to order him away from her

An abused woman asks a judge to issue a court order of protection, a temporary measure that would legally prohibit her batterer from abusing, harassing, or threatening her.

workplace or their children's school. It may give the victim temporary possession of the couple's home and property and require the abuser to pay child support, compensation for losses, and attorney's fees. He may also be required to get counseling or placed on an electronic monitoring device that tracks his movements.

Because orders of protection are often violated, women are advised to carry a copy at all times and to call police immediately if they are approached or threatened by the offender. Even if the orders fail to keep men away from their victims, they increase effective police response. According to one expert, "police tend to respond more supportively towards women who get [protection orders]; perhaps because it signifies to them these women 'mean business.'"[7] Judges also tend to impose harsher sentences on men who violate restraining orders.

Court orders can also be used to protect women whose partners are stalking them. This crime usually occurs after a woman has left her abuser.

Laws against stalking

Stalking is the act of following, watching, or communicating with a person against his or her wishes. It is a threatening behavior that seeks to frighten the victim into submitting to the stalker. Stalkers are obsessed with their victims and often feel their love will overcome the victim's resistance.

When the stalker is a husband or partner, he usually considers the victim to be his property. If she has left him, he will make sure no one else can have her—even if, in some cases, it means killing her. A 1993 report by the Institute of Justice shows that most stalking victims are the former partner of the stalker, and most relationships between stalkers and victims were abusive.

Stalking is a serious crime that sometimes leads to women's deaths. It is also a more difficult crime to prove than battering, as stalkers pursue their victims in secret and those victims do not show signs of physical abuse unless they are attacked.

In 1990 California became the first state to make stalking a crime. All fifty states and the District of Columbia now have antistalking laws, many of which were enacted in the last few years. Some states consider stalking a misdemeanor, punishable by up to 364 days in jail and a fine; in others, it is a felony and carries a sentence of 3 to 5 years. Judges sometimes sentence repeat offenders or especially dangerous stalkers to as many as 20 years in jail.

Stalking victims can get restraining orders against their partners. They must document the threatening behavior, which often includes phone calls, letters, gifts, and vandalism, as well as following or spying, and report it to the police. Even jailed offenders can be charged with stalking if they continue to write to their victims, and their jail sentences will be increased.

Men who violate court orders, whether for battering or for stalking, are subject to arrest. Police in many states are now required to arrest anyone they believe is putting a partner's life in danger.

Protesters rally against domestic violence in Boston. The passage of antistalking and mandatory arrest laws have greatly aided the fight to stop violence against women.

Mandatory arrest of abusers

Mandatory, or required, arrest laws have been enacted in many states during the past few years to allow police officers to arrest abusers without the victim filing charges. Officers instead press charges on behalf of the state. These laws were passed because many abused women fear sending their partners to jail and, thus, refuse to file charges.

Mandatory arrest laws take the burden off abused women by shifting the responsibility for arrest to the police.

Arrested men are less likely to seek revenge if their partners were not the ones who pressed charges, and the women feel less guilt. However, mandatory arrest has become an area of controversy among women. Many feminists oppose it because it takes away the victim's right to choose. It also means that more men are jailed, leaving their families without financial support.

Police officers also have mixed responses to mandatory arrest. On the one hand, they are reluctant to get involved in domestic abuse cases. Many officers feel that a couple should resolve their problems on their own. They believe that police interference is a waste of time when so many women refuse to testify in court against their partners. On the other hand, women who call the police but then fail to press charges often end up calling again the next time they are beaten. Mandatory arrest saves officers repeated visits to the same home.

The role the police play in domestic disputes is a difficult one. It has changed dramatically since the passage of new laws, yet domestic violence calls continue to be the most hated duties of most officers. They are also the largest category of calls received by police departments.

Probable cause for arrest

Police in all states are now required to treat domestic violence as a crime. If they have probable cause, or reason to believe a woman was beaten or is in danger, police in many states must arrest the abuser whether or not the woman consents. The officer's main duty is protecting the safety of the victim.

Officers do not need to witness a crime in order to have probable cause for an arrest. They can base their decision on crime scene observations, including the condition of the home and the state of the people involved. A woman's cuts or bruises, torn clothing, overturned furniture, the presence of weapons, and crying or hiding children are all signs that violence has occurred or been threatened.

If a woman insists that no crime took place—that, for example, she tripped and fell during an argument—the officers have a difficult call to make. Domestic violence is not always obvious. Often both parties have been drinking, a woman may not show signs of physical abuse, and an argument is not by itself cause for arrest. In many cases, concerned or angry neighbors may have called to report a domestic disturbance. Those who blame the police for "doing nothing" often fail to recognize the difficult role they play in these situations.

Assisting the victim

A police officer's job does not end with the arrest. Many offenders are set free on bail until their court date; others may be held overnight, then given a no-contact or seventy-two-hour-stay-away order by a judge to keep them from approaching the victim. With her attacker out of jail, an abused woman is often in danger.

Victims have the right to request police assistance in getting them and their children to a safe place—often a friend's house, a women's shelter, or a motel. Officers are also required to help them get medical care if needed.

Once a woman has been helped to safety, her next step is dealing with the court system. This can be a frightening and confusing experience; without a guiding hand, many women back down from facing their abusers in court.

Treatment of battered women

Until recently, women got very little support from prosecutors (the lawyers representing them in cases against their partners) or the courts. The justice system viewed domestic abuse as out of place in criminal courts, and judges often ordered battered women to make up with their partners. Like police officers, many prosecuting attorneys resented wasting their time with women who withdrew their charges against their abusers. A study in Houston shows that only 6.7 percent of women who showed up at the district attorney's family offense unit with abuse complaints ended up filing charges.

Over the past two decades, supporters of battered women have been pressuring the courts to help women file

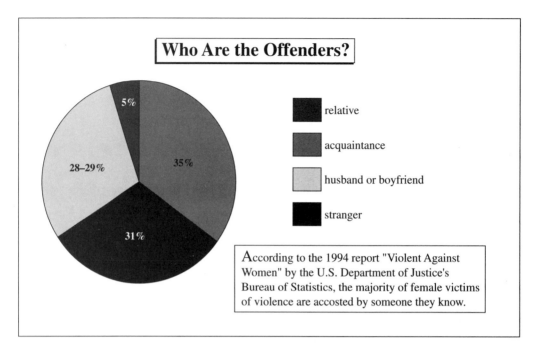

Who Are the Offenders?

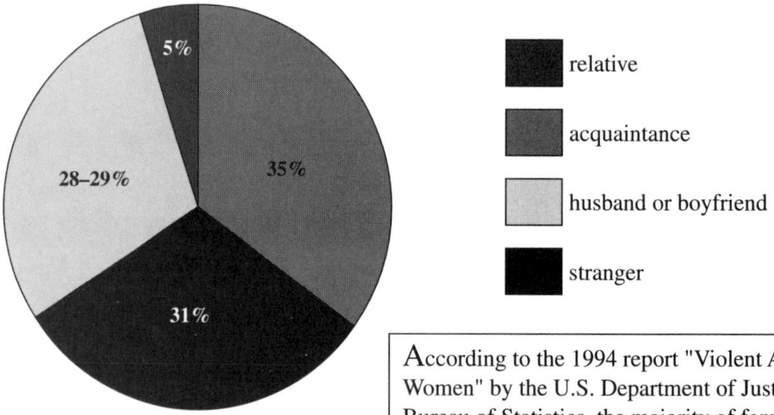

According to the 1994 report "Violent Against Women" by the U.S. Department of Justice's Bureau of Statistics, the majority of female victims of violence are accosted by someone they know.

charges. Women who are assigned counselors to help them fill out forms, explain the legal process, and offer advice and emotional support have a much higher rate of following through. Understanding the reasons for their reluctance to file charges helps these counselors find solutions, such as arranging for temporary shelter or financial aid.

Many people in the justice system recommend that the state, rather than the women themselves, bring charges against abusive partners. As with mandatory arrest, this takes some of the pressure off women and lessens the chances that their abusers will seek revenge; however, many feminists feel that forcing women to prosecute deprives them of their right to decide.

Prosecutors sometimes pressure women into testifying against their partners by charging them with filing false police reports or with perjury, or lying under oath. In rare instances they have even jailed uncooperative victims. Some lawyers feel that letting battered women decide whether to prosecute does not truly give them power when they fear their abusers. As one attorney explains, "When you give the victim control over the criminal prosecution in reality you're giving control to the batterer, because the batterer controls the victim."[8]

Treatment of men accused of abuse

Though men accused of domestic abuse are often found guilty, their sentences tend to be shorter than those of men who commit violence against strangers. Some courts give batterers the option of having the charges against them dropped if they complete a counseling program. Many men who receive jail sentences are also required to attend prevention programs.

The courts have come under strong attack by battered women's advocates, those who fight for the rights of victims of domestic violence. These advocates are particularly critical of judges who sentence abusers to treatment programs instead of jail and grant them generous child visitation rights. Under political pressure from women's groups, many judges are taking a tougher approach, especially when men violate their orders of protection or repeat their crimes.

2

The Nature of Domestic Violence

THERE IS NO single reason why men abuse their partners. Experts disagree on the causes of domestic abuse. Many believe that men learn their abusive behavior from their fathers, while others think certain men are born with the tendency to be violent. Feminists are more likely to blame a society in which men have held most of the power for centuries. Whatever the main cause, there are several factors commonly seen in men in violent relationships. Many experts agree that a man's childhood plays a major role in how he will relate to women as an adult.

From abused child to abusive adult

Experiencing and watching violence in the home has a strong effect on children, who learn about the world from their parents. If those who love a child also hit him, he is likely to grow up thinking that this is an acceptable behavior. Boys who see their fathers getting what they want from family members through violence learn that it is an effective way of meeting their needs. Studies show that witnessing abuse more often leads to adult violence than actually experiencing abuse.

Despite whether a battered child grows up to be an abuser, being abused leaves emotional scars. Many experts see shame as a central factor in boys who become abusers. Boys who are beaten and rejected by their fathers often grow up with little dignity or self-esteem. Physical abuse

Some researchers believe that boys who witness violence in the home may be prone to violence as adults.

does not seem to be as important as emotional abuse, such as being ridiculed in front of others. Boys look to their fathers as role models for developing their identities. When those fathers criticize and humiliate them, they grow up feeling worthless and powerless. Their only sense of power comes from treating others—especially women—the way their fathers treated them.

Random punishment also seems to play a role in the abusive home. Boys who are punished for no apparent reason grow up believing everything they do is wrong; they are unable to separate good behavior from bad. When they become adults and establish relationships with women, they often act in the same unpredictable ways as their fathers, lashing out at small annoyances without warning.

The role played by mothers in abusive homes is less clear. Since they often are abused by their husbands, the mothers of abused boys may be more focused on their own survival than on helping their children. Their sons may grow up blaming them for failing to protect them against their fathers. Battered women often relate to their children in inconsistent ways, showing love and affection when they are not being abused but withdrawing when under attack. Some experts believe this encourages a love-hate attitude in boys who grow up to abuse their partners.

Sons of abusive men often grow up feeling that they have no control over their lives. As they enter adolescence, when gaining control becomes more important, they find that they can control girls the same way they saw their fathers controlling their mothers. Many also start to use alcohol or drugs, which increase the tendency toward violence.

Alcohol and drugs

Alcohol frequently plays a role in domestic violence. Abusive men have a high rate of alcohol use, often linked to depression and anxiety. They often can keep their feelings of anger and frustration in check when they are sober but unleash them when drunk. Many men become violent only while drinking, and they blame the alcohol for their behavior. Some do not even remember what they did while drunk. Heavy binge drinking—drinking a great deal at one time, rather than small amounts regularly—is particularly common in domestic violence situations.

Studies show that the risk of violence increases when the female partners of abusive men also drink. Women under the influence of alcohol are less likely to avoid or walk away from a fight. Abusive men sometimes blame their violence on their partners' drinking or drug use.

Women with alcohol or drug problems are also less able to leave an abusive relationship, as their addiction impairs their judgment and ability to take action. When children are involved, their partners may threaten to take custody by claiming that the women are unfit mothers. These women are often blamed for their problems and receive little help from the justice system. An expert on domestic violence prevention observes that "victims who are drinking are more likely to be blamed for their own victimization; but batterers who are drinking are less likely to be blamed for their violence."[9]

Other drugs can also trigger abuse. Amphetamines, or "uppers," can bring on bursts of violent temper. Cocaine is often seen in abusive homes, and many batterers have problems with drug addiction. All types of drugs that are used to escape from emotional problems tend to make those problems worse, often leading to abusive behavior.

Antisocial personality disorder

Many therapists believe that the most dangerous abusers have a mental illness called antisocial personality disorder. They often have "Jekyll and Hyde" personalities, changing without warning from being pleasant and affectionate to being angry and violent. Men with this disorder are extremely jealous and possessive, need to control others, and belittle their partners. They blame others for their own faults and mistakes. According to a marriage therapist, "They deny what they've done, minimize their attacks, and always blame their victims."[10] They also tend to believe in

The Alcohol Factor

Studies show that incidences of abuse are much higher in families with alcohol problems than in families without. The graphs below compare the abuse rates in both types of families.

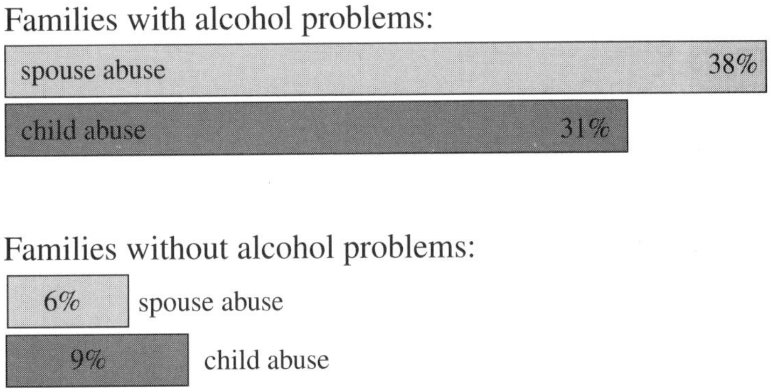

Source: Quoted in Liza N. Burby, *Family Violence*. San Diego: Lucent Books, 1996.

male superiority—that it is natural for men, as the stronger sex, to dominate women.

Men with antisocial personality disorder tend to become obsessed with their partners. Women who leave them are often stalked or threatened.

Experts disagree on whether people are born with this disorder or develop it through years of childhood abuse. Many men with these symptoms come from abusive backgrounds, but it is not clear whether they inherit their violent traits from their fathers or simply learn them.

Other risk factors

Limited education, low income, and poor prospects for advancement can contribute to men's feelings of powerlessness. While domestic violence occurs at all income levels, those with limited resources are more likely to be under stress and have fewer ways to cope with the pressure. The rate of abuse is highest among poor, uneducated men ages eighteen to thirty. A National Family Violence Survey shows that families at or below the poverty level have an abuse rate 500 percent higher than other families. Men who are unemployed and have a large number of children are at particularly high risk of becoming abusive. Also, subcultures among the lower classes, such as street gangs, promote the use of violence and treat women as inferiors.

In addition to having a variety of causes, domestic violence includes several types of abuse, not all of which are physical. They are often used in combination to terrorize women into doing what their partner demands and staying with the abuser.

Battering

Battering covers any physical abuse men inflict on women. It includes hitting, punching, kicking, shoving, twisting arms or legs, scratching, biting, pulling hair, choking, and any other activity that causes physical harm. Battering can also involve the use of weapons.

Battered women are the most obvious victims of domestic violence since their scars are physical. They often have

Battered women usually show signs of their physical abuse, including bruises, cuts, and broken bones.

bruises, cuts, and welts, and victims of severe abuse show up in emergency rooms with broken bones and damaged organs. Some die at the hands of their partners.

Battering frequently follows a cycle in which the abuser's rage builds up over days or weeks, explodes in violence, and then is followed by apologies and expressions of love. There is then a "honeymoon" period during which he is loving and considerate, often bringing his partner gifts, before the anger rebuilds and the abuse begins again. Though there are usually signs that the tension is building, women seldom know what minor event will trigger its release. Batterers sometimes wake their victims from their sleep to beat them, and their violence cannot be controlled. Once the outburst is over, some batterers deny what happened, while others try to win back their victim's love with apologies and promises to change.

Men who beat their partners usually start with minor physical abuse, such as pushing or slapping. Over time their attacks may become more frequent and serious as their need to control increases, often involving weapons.

Because their cases are easier to prove than other forms of abuse, battered women have more success in convincing police and the courts of the crimes committed against them. The more severe the injuries, the more time the abuser is likely to spend in jail. However, men who threaten to harm their partners are sometimes just as dangerous as those who repeatedly beat them.

Threats of violence or death

Many men who beat their partners also try to control them with threats, especially when the women show signs of wanting to leave them. Some use the threat of violence without ever actually following through. Just knowing that a man who is capable of hurting them is considering violence is enough to keep many women in terror, especially if he has guns or knives.

Abusive men often threaten to kill the women they claim to love. Jealousy is the main motive for these threats. They frequently imagine their partner is having an affair with another man and become obsessed with the idea, seeing everything around them as evidence of her guilt. They also fear—often justly—that the women are planning to leave them, and feel that their threats are the only power they have to make them stay.

Some men threaten suicide, murder-suicide, or the killing of the couple's children if their partners abandon them. (Nearly 10 percent of abusers who are abandoned by their partners act on their suicide threats.) Threats involving children are especially terrifying to the women, who often stay with an abusive man for their protection.

All violence and threats involve some type of emotional abuse. Abusers control their victims by frightening them and convincing them that they are helpless without the abuser's "love."

Emotional abuse

Most definitions of domestic violence now include emotional abuse. By itself, emotional abuse is not recognized as a crime by police or the courts; however, this type of abuse usually accompanies physical violence and threats.

Emotional abuse seeks to destroy women's sense of self-esteem, giving their partners psychological power over them. In its extreme form, it is a type of brainwashing or mind control. Emotionally abusive men humiliate their partners and constantly question their intelligence and judgment. They yell at them, call them insulting names, and may accuse them of insanity.

One of the best-known cases of emotional abuse, which was accompanied by brutal physical violence, involved Hedda Nussbaum. She was battered by her partner, Joel Steinberg, for ten years before he was arrested for the beating death of their adopted daughter, Lisa. Steinberg charmed and flattered Nussbaum early in their relationship, then began criticizing her and convincing her she was a bad person who only he could help. In addition to beating her, he convinced her to stay away from her family and friends, caused her to lose her job, and made her dependent on him for money. In her diary, Nussbaum—an intelligent, educated woman who had a successful career before her relationship with Steinberg—wrote, "I must have Joel's love and approval to survive. I'm worthless and helpless."[11]

A police officer escorts Hedda Nussbaum into a police station following the murder of her adopted daughter. Nussbaum's bruised, distorted face shows evidence of her abusive ten-year relationship with Joel Steinberg.

The Nussbaum case is unusual in its degree of violence combined with extreme social control. However, isolating their partners and trying to destroy their self-esteem are common tactics of abusive men.

Isolation is a form of abuse that cuts off women's contacts with the outside world. They have no one to turn to for emotional support except their abusers, who take control of their bodies and minds. Isolated women question their own sanity and come to believe whatever their abusers tell them. They develop symptoms similar to those of people who have been kidnapped and held hostage, identifying with the person who controls their life.

A related form of emotional abuse is deprivation. Along with her other punishments, Hedda Nussbaum was deprived of food and sleep. Her physical state deteriorated to the point where she could not make rational judgments. When her partner was tried for the murder of their child, Nussbaum was judged incapable of either assisting him or protecting the girl.

Why don't these women simply leave their abusers? It is hard for anyone outside the abusive relationship to understand why women stay, particularly when the abuse becomes physical and results in injuries. Women's reasons for remaining are varied and complex.

Women in abusive relationships

Like their partners, many battered women grew up in abusive homes. They may have watched their mothers being beaten and may have been physically and sexually abused themselves. Some of these women also use violence, often against their children. The patterns of behavior they learned as children stay with them as adults.

For people who grew up with violence, reacting physically to family frustrations may seem like a normal response. Women whose fathers drank, shouted, and hit their wives and children are seldom surprised when their partners use the same tactics to get their way.

For other women, the first attack by a partner may be shocking. However, he may beg her forgiveness and promise never to hit her again. He may say he hit her only because he loves her so much and cannot stand it when she looks at another man. This makes her feel loved and needed, so she forgives him. And each time the abuse recurs, she wants to believe it is the last.

The batterer may convince his partner she is the only one who understands him and can help him. As one expert says, "Many battered women believe they are the sole support of the batterer's emotional stability and sanity, the one link their men have to the normal world. Sensing the batterer's isolation and despair, they feel responsible for his well-being."[12]

Many people blame battered women for their situation. No one forced them to get involved with an abusive man, they argue, and no one is forcing them to stay with him. This position oversimplifies a complicated issue.

Blaming the victim

For many years it was common to blame women for their abuse. Police, the courts, and public opinion saw battered women as self-made victims. They were blamed for provoking violence by disobeying their husbands, and many saw wife abuse as a just form of discipline.

Battered women often suffer from feelings of isolation that keep them from leaving their abusive partners.

Even today, after all the changes of the past two decades, there is a tendency to blame the victim. After all, it takes two to fight. Many people reason that if these women did not behave in a certain way, their partners' rage would not follow. What disproves this argument is that when a woman leaves her abuser—as women often do—he quickly finds another victim. Abusive men are violent against any women who are unfortunate enough to cross their paths.

Women are also blamed for not leaving their attackers; however, many obstacles exist, including the very realistic fear of being pursued and killed. Leaving any intimate relationship is difficult; leaving an abusive one is frightening and dangerous. Battered women often have been stripped of economic and social support as well as their self-esteem.

There are many ties that bind women to their abusers, and a large percentage of women never leave their abusive relationship. Their reasons for staying can be social, economic, self-preserving, and emotional.

Social pressures to stay married

Leaving an abusive husband was more difficult years ago, when divorce was seen as something shameful. Today, half of all marriages end in divorce. Still, in many sectors of American society there is strong pressure to stay married, especially if a couple has children. And the pressure is usually on women to make the marriage work.

Among traditional groups, including many recent immigrants, there are strong religious and cultural pressures to keep a marriage intact. These groups also hold traditional ideas about male and female roles, and wives are still expected to serve and obey their husbands. As a result, rates of wife abuse are high, yet women seldom feel free to escape. A social worker who counsels Cambodian women in the United States notes, "The stigma of divorce and fear of bringing shame upon the family is especially hard for them to deal with. Everything belongs to the husband, is his property—assets, wife, and kids. . . . Violence is viewed as a means to control and is not seen as a problem."[13]

Women who have recently immigrated to the United States have special problems with domestic violence. They rarely have anyplace to turn for help. In addition to their fear of disobeying their husbands, they often speak little English, are afraid of being deported, and have no financial resources. Even if these women dare to leave an abusive husband, they have few marketable skills and can rarely earn a living on their own.

Economic need

Men in abusive homes often control the family finances. They may prohibit their wives from working, keep all bank accounts and credit cards exclusively in their name, and give their partners small allowances that cover only their basic needs. Establishing a new life without money or credit is extremely hard; added to all the other problems of leaving an abuser, they make it close to impossible.

Most women who stay with an abusive partner have at least one child. Escaping with children is especially difficult without financial support. Women who leave their children behind may be charged with desertion or endangerment and risk losing custody.

Many abused women are unemployed, have no property in their own name, and have little money and no credit history. Some researchers have found that the biggest factor in a woman's leaving her abuser is having the economic resources to survive on her own. Those who succeed in breaking the ties with their partner usually have researched their financial situation and the law.

Another reason women have trouble leaving an abusive relationship is fear. Many women are afraid they will be followed and physically harmed or that they will lose custody of their children if they are seen as either abandoning or kidnapping them.

Fear of being stalked

Escaping a violent man is dangerous. Many women fear that their partners will track them down and hurt or even kill them, and their fears are justified. One study showed that 45 percent of women's murders result from a man's rage over his partner's leaving or threatening to leave him. Each year, according to the FBI, about three thousand men kill their current or former wives or girlfriends.

The most dangerous time for battered women is when they escape their abusers. These men have lost the one thing

Leaving an Abusive Relationship

Unfortunately, many women who leave their batterers continue to be at risk for domestic violence.

- Approximately 75 percent of all emergency room visits by battered women occur after they have separated from their batterers.
- Approximately 75 percent of requests for law enforcement assistance in a domestic situation occur during separation.
- Approximately 50 percent of all murders involving wives or girlfriends occur after they leave their batterers.

Source: Family Violence Awareness Page.

in their lives they were able to control, and they are desperate to get it back. Some of them will go to any length to find where their partners have moved, including hiring detectives, confronting the victim's friends, and lying about their own identity to get confidential information.

Women who lack a strong support system, such as family and friends who can help protect them against their partner, are more fearful of leaving. Because abusers try to isolate their partners from friends and family, many women find themselves alone with their problems. With no one to advise them, they are unaware of the social agencies and programs that help battered women find safety and rebuild their lives.

The fear of attack extends to a battered woman's children. Whether she flees with them or leaves them with her partner, their lives may be in danger. Abandoned partners sometimes threaten to kill their children, often at the same time they are threatening suicide.

Fear of losing children

Batterers often use children as bargaining chips with their partners. They may threaten to file for custody if the woman leaves them, and they sometimes succeed. In rare cases, even men who were convicted of killing their wives have been awarded custody of their children. In an Illinois case, James Lutgen served less than three years for strangling his wife, Carol, to death in front of their daughters. Upon his release from jail he was judged "a fit and proper parent to have care and control of his minor children."[14] The judge felt that the best place for the children was with their natural father, even though they had witnessed him killing their mother.

While women who leave their children with their abuser may be charged with child endangerment, those who remove them from the home may be charged with kidnapping. Crossing state borders with children to flee an abuser is illegal in some parts of the country. Unless women know their rights, hire an attorney, and follow proper legal procedures, they run the risk of losing their children or even going to jail.

A mother and daughter sit in the safety of a battered women's shelter. Many women fear that their batterers will retaliate with violence against their children or sue for custody if they leave the abusive relationship.

The emotional bond between abuser and victim

Even women who have educational, social, and financial resources have emotional attachments to their abusers that make it hard to leave. A battered woman may feel she is the only person in the world who can help her partner, who may have a problem with alcohol or drugs. In many cases both partners were abused as children, and their shared pasts may create a strong emotional bond between them.

Many abusive men seem to have two personalities. Between bouts of violent rage, they may be charming and romantic and seem to love their partner. They may apologize after their attack, crying and pleading for forgiveness. These men often blame their drinking or drug problem and promise to get help—and they may even go for counseling, if only briefly. Their partners want so much to believe in their promises that they forget how many times they have been broken over the years.

Some severely battered women have lost their own identity and cannot imagine life without their partner. They have given up their opinions, friends, and job to try to please him and keep the peace. They hope that if they meet his standards, the abuse will stop. And since the batterer expects his partner to anticipate and meet all his needs perfectly—an impossible standard—the abuse is endless.

In extreme cases of abuse the victim may lose touch with reality. Hedda Nussbaum suffered a ruptured spleen, numerous broken bones, a severely damaged eye, burns, and countless other injuries at the hands of her abuser. Yet she said after her partner was jailed, "I didn't see myself as battered. To me, the beatings were isolated incidents. I always thought each one was the last. I loved Joel so much. I always felt there was more good between us than not."[15]

3

Rape

MILLIONS OF WOMEN have been raped throughout history by their partners, by acquaintances, and by strangers. While rape is a sexual act, it is driven more by anger than by sexual desire. Rapists attack their victims to exercise control over them. By forcing women to submit to their wishes, they gain a false, temporary sense of power.

Rape has been used for centuries to shame, dishonor, and oppress not only women but also their partners and societies. It has been used as a weapon in war, in which bands of soldiers have invaded villages and raped women to dishonor the enemy. In some societies women are forced to marry their rapists to avoid bringing further shame upon their families.

Until recently, rape was a crime whose victims were shamed into silence. Women were often treated as though they, rather than their attackers, had committed a crime. They were discouraged from going to trial against their rapists, whose defense attorneys argued that the women had been seeking sex. Some of these women are finally speaking out years after their trials, showing that it is the rapists, and not their victims, who need to be ashamed.

A great deal of attention has been focused in recent years on date rape, in which the victim knows her attacker and may even have a relationship with him. This crime was rarely reported in the past because its victims were not believed. Many women who pressed charges against their attackers felt they had been raped twice—first by the rapist, then by the courts.

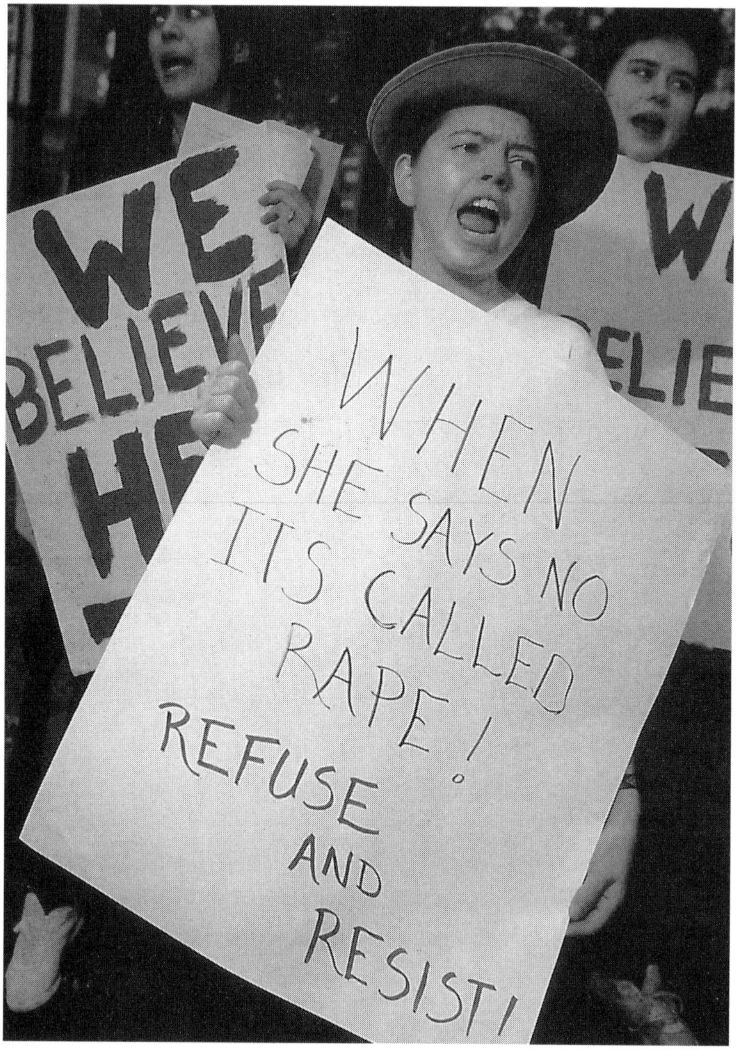

Protesters demonstrate outside of a date rape trial. Increasing numbers of rape victims are speaking out against such violence and taking their attackers to court.

Date rape and acquaintance rape

Among the many myths about rape, perhaps the most misleading is that most rapists are crazy loners who jump out of the shadows at unsuspecting women. Most rapists know their victims, and many have intimate relationships with them. Women are four times more likely to be raped by a boyfriend or acquaintance than by a stranger.

In 1985, *Ms.* magazine did a study of over six thousand college students on thirty-two campuses across the country to gather statistics on date and acquaintance rape. They found that one in four women reported being the victim of rape or attempted rape, that 84 percent of them knew their attackers, and that 57 percent of the rapes had occurred on dates. Many victims had never reported their attacks to the police, and many were unaware that date rape is a crime. As the director of a rape education organization reported, "Because sexually coercive behavior is so common in our male-female interactions, rape by an acquaintance may not be perceived as rape."[16]

In the years since the *Ms.* study, awareness of date and acquaintance rape has greatly increased, particularly on college campuses. Women are now much more likely to file charges against their attackers, just as police are more likely to arrest them and the courts to prosecute them. However, acquaintance and date rape are still widely committed and greatly underreported, and men still commonly argue that they simply misunderstood what their victims wanted.

Mixed signals: the issue of consent

Much date and acquaintance rape is based on—though not excused by—miscommunication. Men and women often interpret behavior and signals differently, with men more ready to read sexual meaning into a woman's words or actions. Many men invite women out only after they have decided they want to have sex with them, while women tend to view dates as opportunities to get to know the men better. Even if they try to make this clear, many men are conditioned to ignore what women say and want. A male college student described the situation with this sharp observation:

> The man is taught to look upon his actions on a date as a carefully constructed strategy for gaining the most territory. Every action is evaluated in terms of the final goal—intercourse. He continually pushes to see "how far he can get." He knows—she will probably say "no." But he has learned to separate himself from her interests. He is more concerned with winning the game.[17]

Some men believe that rape is justified in certain situations, though they seldom call it by that name. They think that men have the right to have sex with a woman who asks them on a date, behaves or dresses in a way that suggests that she wants to have sex, or goes to a man's home. A survey of high school boys shows that 54 percent thought rape was justified when a girl "led a boy on." In their minds, women give up the right to say "no" once they have given signals that they might mean "yes." In the words of the same college student, "When she finally says 'No,' he simply may not listen, or he may convince himself that she really means

A majority of high school boys who took part in one survey believed rape was justified in certain situations, particularly when a girl dressed or acted in a misleading manner.

'yes.' With such a miserable failure rate in communication, a man can rape a woman even when she is resisting vocally and physically, and still believe that it was not rape."[18]

Because women are brought up not to use force, or even to express their wishes forcefully, they may not fight back or show signs of resisting. Their attackers, determined to get what they want, tune out the women's words and interpret their lack of resistance as acceptance. When the rapist is someone a woman knows and has agreed to be with, she is less likely to protest loudly. She is often confused, doubts her interpretation of what is happening, and blames herself for getting caught in the situation or even for bringing it about.

Drugs or alcohol can complicate the situation even further. People whose judgment is clouded cannot safely determine sexual consent.

Complicating factors: alcohol and drugs

In the *Ms.* study, 75 percent of the men and 55 percent of the women involved in acquaintance or date rape had been drinking or taking drugs just before the attack. Alcohol and drugs distort reality, impair judgment, and slow reactions. People who are using them often expose themselves to dangers they would otherwise avoid and are less able to defend themselves when threatened.

Some men use alcohol as an excuse for raping women. They blame it for causing both their own aggressive behavior and what they interpret as a woman's consent. A woman who is drunk is less able to fend off a sexual attack and may not even be completely aware it is taking place. Many rapes on college campuses involve women who are too drunk to legally consent to having sex; in some cases they are attacked after they have passed out from drinking.

Many illegal drugs also reduce women's ability to make rational decisions about having sex. Some of these drugs have been used in date rape scenarios.

Rohypnol: the "date rape" drug

A new factor in date rape is the recent discovery by sexually abusive men of the drug Rohypnol. Rohypnol, which dissolves easily in drinks, causes sleepiness, muscle relaxation, loss of motor control, and memory loss. Men who slip it into their dates' drinks have the perfect rape victim: someone powerless to fight back, who often is not even aware of being raped until afterward.

Although Rohypnol is illegal in the United States, many Americans have been getting the drug from other countries, particularly Mexico. Other drugs that have similar effects, Ketamine and GBH, have also become popular, especially on college campuses. Since the use of "date rape" drugs is recent, the extent of the problem is not known.

The abuse of these drugs is a frightening new development for women. Precautions like limiting their alcohol intake and avoiding dangerous situations, such as going alone to a man's apartment, are no longer enough in defending against date rape. Women are being warned to keep an eye on their drinks to be sure they are not tampered with by a potential rapist.

There is widespread agreement that rape of all kinds is a serious crime and that drugs like Rohypnol are terrible weapons against women. However, many people believe that the movement to fight rape has gone overboard in defining rape and in making women look like victims in society.

The feminist debate on women as victims

The 1985 *Ms.* magazine survey, which reported that one in four women on college campuses had been the victim of acquaintance rape or attempted rape, sparked a strong anti-rape campaign by feminist groups. Posters with this alarming one-in-four statistic warned women on campuses across the country that they were likely to become victims. However, many women, including feminists, disagree both with the study's findings and with its message. It suggested that women were powerless against men's advances and needed special protection. Writer Katie Roiphe, a college student at the time, wrote that "campus feminists produce endless images of women as victims—women offended by a professor's dirty joke, women pressured into sex by peers, women trying to say no but not getting it across."[19]

A major objection is to the way the study defined rape. The statistics on rape victims included women who felt pressured—not necessarily forced or threatened—into having sex while drinking or taking drugs. They would not meet the legal definition of rape victims. This broadened view of rape is expressed by feminist legal scholar Catharine MacKinnon: "Politically, I call it rape whenever a woman has had sex and feels violated."[20]

More important, however, is the way the *Ms.* report, as well as the arguments of many feminists during the 1980s, portrays women as victims. In Roiphe's words, "If we assume that women are not all helpless and naïve, then they should be responsible for their choice to drink or take drugs. If a woman's 'judgment is impaired' and she has sex, it isn't always the man's fault; it isn't always rape."[21] She worries that women, who fought for decades to achieve the political and economic power they have today, risk losing it by portraying themselves as weak and fragile: "Rape-crisis feminists threaten the progress that's been made. They are chasing the same stereotypes that our mothers spent so much energy escaping."[22]

Critics of the Ms. *rape survey assert that portraying women as helpless victims insults not only women's strength but also their judgment and intelligence.*

In destroying the old myths about rape, "rape-crisis" feminists are accused of starting new ones. In literature and courses given on campuses, these feminists argue that women who have been drinking are incapable of consenting to sex and that unless a woman clearly states that she wants it, any sexual act that takes place is rape. To many women, this is a big step backward and insults women's intelligence and strength.

Rape within marriage

While feminists have focused much of their attention on date rape, another area where traditional ideas have changed is forced sex within marriage. It is seldom reported and even more rarely prosecuted, yet rape within marriage is a serious and often violent crime.

Like some women who are raped on dates, many women who are raped by their husbands do not know they are victims of a crime. Some men feel they have a right to sex on demand from their wives, an idea going back to the days when women were their husbands' property. Marital rape is a crime in only seventeen countries throughout the world, and not all states in the United States have laws protecting women from forced sex within marriage.

There are no reliable statistics on rape within marriage because the crime is so seldom reported. In a 1992–93 Marital Crime Victimization Survey, a half million American women reported having been raped or sexually assaulted by their husband, though few had filed charges. A recent survey shows that 5 percent of rapes or sexual assaults are committed by husbands or ex-husbands of the victim. Some researchers report that 10 to 14 percent of women are raped by their husbands; others show figures as high as 25 percent.

Reporting marital rape

Marital rape usually surfaces only when its victims are severely beaten. Even then they often seek medical help for their injuries but fail to report the rape. Close to half of reported rapes by husbands involve battering. Alcohol abuse is a common factor in many of these assaults. Of the nearly half of marital rapes that do not involve battering, a researcher observes, "These rapes seemed to be motivated less by anger than by a desire to assert power, establish control, teach a lesson, show who was boss."[23]

While marital rape is now a crime in all states, thirty-three states require that it involve a husband using force against his wife unless the woman was legally unable to consent, such as because of a disability. When women report marital rape to the police, they often are not taken seriously. A 1996 study shows that 80 percent of women who called the police about their assaults were dissatisfied with the response.

Date, acquaintance, and marital rape are all serious crimes that can leave long-term emotional scars on their victims. However, the most feared type of sexual assault is rape by strangers.

Rape by strangers

When people picture rape, the image is usually of stranger rape: women assaulted at random by men they have never met, often with a history of criminal violence. While stranger rapes are greatly outnumbered by acquaintance or partner rapes, they are among the most terrifying of all crimes.

Women who do not know their attackers are completely at their mercy. Unlike date rape, stranger rape involves no issues of consent or miscommunication. The attacker is out to rape and has no concern for his victim; he does not know her and will not have to deal with her afterward. The woman has no idea how he will react if she resists or tries to reason with him—he is a stranger, whose personality and history are a blank to her. She only knows that she must act quickly, relying on her instinct to avoid danger or even death.

Facts About Rape

- 25 percent of rapes take place in a public area.
- 68 percent of rapes occur between 6 A.M. and 6 P.M.
- At least 45 percent of rapists are under the influence of drugs or alcohol.
- Rapists use weapons in 29 percent of rapes.
- 75 percent of victims require medical attention after the rape.
- Only 26 percent of all rapes and attempted rapes are reported to the police.

Source: Bureau of Statistics, U.S. Dept. of Justice, 1994.

Stranger rapes are the most vigorously prosecuted sexual attacks and the most likely to get sympathy for the victim from a jury. Many of the attackers are serial, or repeat, rapists who have been convicted of other violent crimes, and many are wanted by the police for other rapes. Previous crimes help lengthen their jail sentences when they are convicted.

Rape in the courts

Before the 1970s the courts required physical evidence of sexual assault to try a rape case. This put a greater burden on rape victims than on victims of other violent crimes, such as robbery and attempted murder. Prosecutors had to have proof of the attacker's identity, along with evidence that sex and force had been used. Because many rapists disguised themselves with masks before their attacks, prosecution was often impossible. Linda Fairstein, an assistant district attorney in New York City, notes, "Thus, in this most intimate of all assaults, the crime least likely to be witnessed by anyone, the overwhelming percentage of victims were legally barred from ever presenting their stories to a jury."[24]

In 1972 the FBI estimated that only one in ten female rape victims reported her attack. When they did press charges, these women were unlikely to get a conviction. Victims were reluctant to discuss the intimate details of their attacks in court. Defense attorneys were allowed to expose the women's pasts to use against them, encouraging juries to believe that the victims had invited their rapists to have sex. Confused juries had trouble understanding the rapists' motives and often set them free.

During the 1970s victims also had to appear at a preliminary hearing where they were forced to face their attackers. Fear of seeing their rapists again was enough to discourage many women from testifying against them in court.

Changing the treatment of victims

Under pressure from women's groups, major changes were made to the laws in the mid-1970s. Prosecutors could present cases without physical evidence of rape, so a woman too frightened to go right to the police after her attack was no longer denied a trial. As a result, rape conviction rates went up.

Many cities established divisions within the court systems to help rape victims through the legal process. New York City started its Sex Crimes Protection Unit in 1974, the first of its kind in the country. This unit recognized that "sex offenses occupy a unique place in the criminal justice system because of the more traumatic nature of the crimes, the most personal invasions an individual can sustain."[25] It let rape victims be interviewed in a private setting by lawyers trained to meet their special needs and provided medical attention and counseling. In the unit's first year of operation, conviction rates tripled.

Rape counselors can help women who are going to trial against their rapists locate support services and navigate their way through the legal system.

Another major advance for rape victims' rights is legal protection against abusive practices in court by defense lawyers. Before rape shield laws were passed, many victims were afraid to press charges because of the way their lives could be destroyed on the witness stand.

Rape shield laws

Defense attorneys used to get away with portraying rape victims as "bad" women who lured the defendants into having sex with them. Linda Fairstein recalls her shock when, prosecuting the brutal rapist of a young woman in the 1970s, the defendant's attorney attacked the victim's character, using her underwear as evidence: "The lawyer dangled the underwear in front of the jurors, demanded of them to consider the type of woman who would purchase and wear that kind of panties: 'Not a businesswoman, not a lady . . . but a hooker.' "[26]

At that time, almost anything in a woman's past could be used against her in court, including the details of all her prior relationships. Women's groups were outraged by this practice of publicly blaming and humiliating the victim, particularly when the attackers' prior crimes often could not be mentioned in court because they might prejudice the jury. Throughout the nation they pushed for the creation of rape shield laws—laws that prevent defense attorneys from presenting information about the victim that does not relate directly to the case.

Improved testing for rape

Police medical examiners have improved their techniques for testing for evidence of rape over the past few years. DNA sperm tests can now show with near certainty the person with whom a victim has had sexual contact. With this genetic proof, rapists can no longer get away with denying their sexual participation; their only hope is that a jury will believe that the woman consented. Bruises or other signs of force make it unlikely that a jury will believe their claims of innocence.

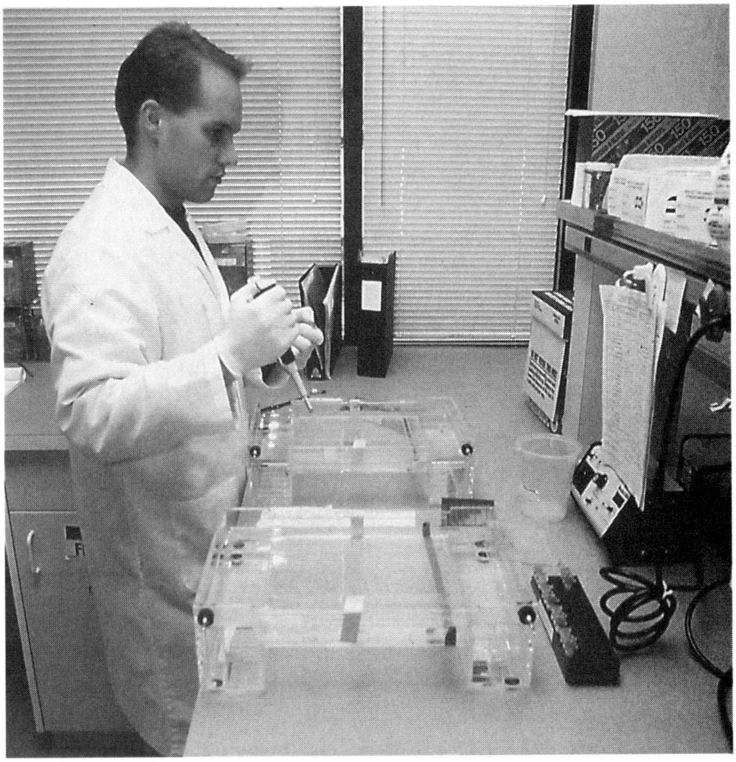

A lab technician prepares samples of DNA. Improved DNA testing methods can now identify rapists with near certainty as well as vindicate men wrongly accused of the crime.

This testing also helps men who have been wrongly accused of rape. Some men who spent many years in prison have been released due to improvements in DNA testing since their cases were tried. According to the director of the Innocence Project at the Benjamin Cardozo School of Law, about one-third of men whose sperm was tested for DNA in sexual assault cases were proven to be the wrong suspect. For women, convicting the wrong man means the real rapist is free to commit more crimes.

These advances have led to more rape victims reporting their crimes, being willing to testify against their attackers, and getting convictions. However, new laws and tougher enforcement have not had a clear effect on reducing the number of rapes that are committed. Rape continues to be a widespread problem in the United States. Many women feel that, along with other forms of violence against women, it will continue on a large scale until attitudes toward women in American culture change.

4

Sex and Violence in American Culture

MANY FEMINISTS, AS well as others, believe that violence against women, particularly sexual assault, is related to the way women are shown in popular culture. They feel that movies, television, advertising, and popular music all influence the way people think about men and women. By portraying powerful men controlling weak women, and by making the use of force look glamorous, many media producers help shape the way men and women view their roles in society.

Although many people agree that the media play a role in how men and women see themselves and each other, widespread disagreement exists about whether media images of sex and violence lead men to abuse women. Studies on the relationship between watching images of sex and violence and actual crime show differing results and lack enough evidence to draw solid conclusions.

The feminist view: violence against women as a reflection of society

Most feminists are critical of the ways women are shown in the media. These images tend to fall into two categories: "good girls," who submit to men's wishes and do not seem to have minds of their own, and "bad girls," who behave more like men—and are punished for doing so. They are largely images created by men, and many feminists argue that they are distorted male fantasies of women.

For years these images have influenced the attitudes of millions of viewers. They have changed over time to reflect social change, but the basic images remain the same. Men are shown in positions of power, whether controlling Western towns with their guns or controlling their families at home, and women who question that power usually come to a bad end.

Many feminists believe that men commit violent acts against women because they have been programmed since childhood to see women as victims. The images that surround them, from television screens to billboard ads, show powerful men controlling women. The women's only power is in being seductive, leading men to view them as objects for their sexual pleasure. Because they are "objects," these women are not seen as having thoughts or feelings of their own. Men see them as extensions of themselves, designed to meet their needs. When the women refuse to submit to these needs, they may be punished—verbally abused, raped, and beaten.

Women in New York City protest against Sports Illustrated, *contending that the magazine's annual swimsuit issue portrays women as sexual objects.*

However, not all feminists support this view. If the media program men to be violent toward women, they argue, why aren't most men abusive? Also, the idea that American culture makes men violent takes away their own responsibility for their acts. It puts the blame on society, not on the men who rape, beat, or murder women.

Not only feminists are concerned about images of sex and violence in the media. Many studies suggest—though do not prove—a link between crime and the amount of aggression watched on television and in movies. These studies have led to calls for censorship from a wide range of groups, from feminists to concerned parents to right-wing religious organizations. They have led to heated debates on free speech and the First Amendment, the law that protects it even when it offends certain parts of society.

Much of this debate centers on two media forms most likely to be viewed by boys: movies and television. The high viewership of young male audiences has helped shape the content of these types of popular entertainment.

Sex and violence in movies and television

Because young male audiences are so large in number, movie and television producers gear much of their programming to what they think teenage boys would like to see. This, many critics argue, leads to unrealistic images of women. These women tend to be fantasy figures—young, beautiful, and submissive women who idolize men or, if they refuse to, are put in their place, often with violence.

Action-adventure movies, which are packed with violent images, are filled with these female fantasy figures. Many of these women, who dress and act in a sexually provocative way, are "bad girls" who have to be overpowered or killed off. The very popular James Bond movies have always featured such women—beautiful villains who try to lure the hero into their evil web. This tradition has continued with the screen versions of adventure comic books such as the Batman movies.

In addition to this distorted view of women, sex and violence are often blended on-screen in ways that make rape appear romantic. Scenes of men and women fighting, in which the men win the struggle and force the women to submit to their sexual demands, are common. Unlike real life, the women do not end up battered and sobbing; they instead appear grateful that the men convinced them of what they really want—to be overpowered. A classic scene in the 1939 movie *Gone With the Wind* illustrates this, with the dashing Rhett Butler battling the willful Scarlett O'Hara, then sweeping her up a staircase toward the bedroom. The message to viewers is that she got what she secretly wanted.

As images of sex and violence become more common on television, many parents worry that children will be encouraged to imitate the violence or will become desensitized to it.

Television has always been subject to greater censorship than movies because of its access to very young viewers. Images of sex and violence are less graphic than in movies, though they have become much more so in recent years. This increase in sexual and violent content has led to protest from parents and religious groups, resulting in an extension of the rating system first applied to movies. It has also led to the recent development of "V-chips," devices that let parents block certain programming from being watched by their children.

Television's influence

Despite these efforts, most children view a great deal of programming with sexual and violent content. Much of this is hidden in Saturday morning cartoons. Because their action heroes are comic-book figures, parents are usually less concerned about the influence they have on children. However, these cartoons are filled with grossly exaggerated, nonstop violence, and many argue that its unrealistic nature leads children to have an unrealistic view of the pain and suffering violence causes. They also show extreme fantasy images of women, with impossible body

Reprinted by permission of Ed Gamble.

proportions and sexually provocative costumes. This blend of violence and sexual suggestion in programming for preteen viewers is of great concern to people who believe childhood images shape developing minds.

Recent surveys show that the average child will watch one hundred thousand acts of violence on television before graduating from elementary school. On Saturday morning, a prime viewing time for children, network programs average twenty-five acts of violence an hour, double the rate in the early 1970s.

Because children watch so much television, often without supervision, there is widespread concern about the amount of violence in television programs. Even when victims are not female characters, many critics believe that the constant viewing of violence causes children to become insensitive to its effect in real life. Young children often have trouble separating fantasy from reality, and they may not recognize the seriousness of violence in real life when it is treated so casually on-screen. There is also concern that boys, seeing male television characters get what they want through violent acts, will imitate this behavior.

A new study by the National Cable Television Association found that 57 percent of cable and broadcast programs contain violent scenes and that one-third of those include nine or more violent incidents. Researchers reported that TV characters who commit violence are seldom punished. Nearly half the time, violent acts on television do not show the injuries suffered by victims, and 58 percent of victims show no pain. Many researchers are convinced of a strong link between watching television violence and aggressive behavior, especially among boys. Teachers and others who work with children tend to agree. A school health coordinator who taught for twenty-two years observed, "For a kid to slap or push another kid down doesn't mean what it used to. They're desensitized because of what they see on TV."[27]

Even if parents are able to control what their children see in movies and on television, they cannot keep them from seeing offensive advertising. Billboards, magazines, and even the sides of buses show disturbing images that suggest sex and violence.

Glamorized images of women as victims in advertising and popular music

To many critics, advertising is one of the worst offenders in creating negative images of women. Since it aims to instantly capture the viewer's attention, its images tend to be provocative. Advertisers often use shock appeal—disturbing images that keep the viewer from turning the page of a magazine or walking past a billboard. The suggestion of sex and violence is a common technique in recent advertising campaigns,

One of the manufacturers most criticized for his advertising programs is the designer Calvin Klein. His use of what appear to be adolescent models, underdressed and in sexually suggestive poses, has outraged many feminists and other critics. Underwear ads featuring the young, shockingly thin model Kate Moss—who appeared to many to be in her early teens—drew outrage for their suggestion of child pornography. His ads for the perfume Obsession show a childlike bare-breasted model with bruised-looking eyes, suggesting a victim of sexual abuse. Klein himself, who was forced to withdraw later ads that were even more disturbing, admitted in a 1988 interview about his advertising images, "I've done everything I could in a provocative sense without being arrested."[28]

A teacher who produced a video lecture critical of the advertising industry noted that the average American is exposed to about fifteen hundred ads a day. Commenting on ads portraying women as objects, she says, "turning a human being into a thing is almost always the first step toward justifying violence against that person."[29]

The fashion industry has always aimed to startle audiences. Perhaps more than any other business, its products must strike the viewer as new. However, many people feel that in recent years it has crossed certain lines with its suggestion of sex mixed with violence. The late designer Gianni Versace dressed models in what looked like leather bondage, outfits that suggested being tied up and beaten. His recently popular "heroin chic" look showed starved-looking models with dark circles under their eyes, suggesting vulnerable, drug-addicted victims of abuse.

Not all media images mixing sex with violence are visual. The music industry has also followed the trend toward showing women as victims in recent years.

Designer Calvin Klein's ads showing youthful models in provocative poses have been criticized for glamorizing child pornography.

Several forms of music popular among the young have strong antiwoman themes, and music videos often feature women as sex objects or victims of abuse. Much heavy metal and hardcore punk rock music has themes of murder, torture, and rape. Some album covers show women tied up and degraded, sometimes wearing dog collars and being treated like animals. A study of music videos by the *Journal of Broadcasting and Electronic Media* showed that in a random sample of sixty-two MTV videos, over half contained scenes of violence and crime.

The recent popularity of "gangsta rap" has drawn strong protest from women's groups and others for its themes of violence and hate. Lyrics by such groups as the Ghetto Boys express anger and violence toward women: "Her body's so beautiful so I'm thinking rape / Shouldn't have had her curtains open so that's her fate. . . . Slit her throat and watched her shake."[30]

Many people believe this music, and the videos that accompany it, promote sexist attitudes and violence toward women. A study in *Psychology of Women Quarterly* reports that men who listened to heavy metal music showed negative attitudes toward women and a greater acceptance of violence. The deputy medical director of the American Psychiatric Association notes, "The American Psychiatric Association believes that violent and demeaning musical lyrics have a deleterious effect on our youth and place at grave risk the mental health and welfare of themselves and our communities."[31]

The record industry has come under attack for producing the work of men who promote hatred, violence, and the victimization of women. Though they defend their albums as free artistic expression, some producers have dropped certain performers because of bad publicity and the threat of boycotts by women. The main target of many women's protests, however, has been pornography.

The debate on pornography

Pornography is defined as any material whose main purpose is to arouse sexual desire. Most pornography is directed toward men and involves images of women. There has been much legal debate over the years about what material is considered pornographic—having no other value than to excite—as well as whether such material should be banned.

People who oppose pornography believe that it causes its audience to view women as sexual objects rather than complete human beings. Many feel that it is not only demeaning to women but also leads men to commit sex crimes against them.

Though there is little evidence that reading or watching pornography causes men to commit crimes, some sex offenders have used this in their defense. Many people fighting to outlaw pornography point to serial rapist and murderer Ted Bundy, whose cross-country crime spree ended the lives of dozens of young women. From his prison cell on Death Row, Bundy blamed pornography for bringing out his uncontrollable urges to rape and kill. He commented, "I've met a lot of men who were motivated to commit violence like me. And without exception, every one of them was deeply involved in pornography."[32]

Evaluating cause and effect

Although studies do not prove a direct cause and effect, they do show that many violent sex offenders read or view pornographic material before committing their crimes. An FBI study indicates that as many as 81 percent of men convicted of sex crimes fit this pattern. Another study, by the Michigan State Police, shows that 41 percent of sex crimes were committed by men who had just viewed pornography and concluded: "Violent pornography is like a how-to manual for rapists and child abusers."[33]

In 1984 the government set up a commission to investigate links between pornography and criminal behavior. An earlier national commission in 1970 had been unable to establish such a link, but the Meese Commission sought to overturn its findings. Its report concluded that "exposure to sexually violent materials has indicated an increase in the likelihood of aggression. More specifically, the research

. . . shows a causal relationship between exposure of this type and aggressive behavior towards women."[34]

However, the methods of the Meese Commission were strongly criticized. At its first hearing, the commission heard from forty-two pornography opponents and only three people who defended it as free speech. Other studies have also been criticized, both for their methods and their conclusions.

People who defend pornography point to the countries in which it is widespread and have low rates of violent sex crime. The rate of rape has declined in West Germany since pornographic material became widely available in 1973. A similar drop was seen in Denmark. And in Japan, where violent pornography is common, the rape rate is much lower than in the United States, where it is restricted. Some of the highest rates of violence against women are in Islamic countries, which forbid pornography. Some researchers

even argue that pornography lowers crime rates because it gives men an outlet for their sexual and violent urges. They feel that in acting out through fantasy, these men will lose the need to commit sex crimes.

Even feminists are strongly divided on the effects of pornography. Some point out that only a small percentage of pornographic material includes violent content. However, others believe that all pornography, regardless of whether it shows violence against women, is degrading and promotes harmful attitudes. In 1983 two of pornography's leading opponents, Catharine MacKinnon and Andrea Dworkin, drafted a law against any material that presents women "dehumanized as sexual objects" or "in scenarios of degradation."[35] The law was rejected in most cities that tried to pass it. Though it did pass in Indianapolis in 1984, it was struck down in federal court as violating the First Amendment.

Victimization and addiction

The pornography that comes under the strongest attack blends sex with violence, almost always with women as victims. Many women were outraged by the positive reviews of the recent movie *The People vs. Larry Flynt*, about the career of *Hustler* magazine's publisher. The film, which shows Flynt's court victory in defending his right to publish pornography, was seen by many as a celebration of First Amendment rights. What angered so many women was what the film did not show: that *Hustler*'s focus is not limited to nudity and sex, but extends to photos of women being chained, beaten, humiliated, and seriously hurt.

The studies that make the strongest case against pornography show that certain men become addicted to it. They develop a need to view pornographic material more and more often, and the type of pornography becomes more graphic and violent over time. Other studies show an increase in aggressive behavior among young men who watch scenes of sex and violence over a long period. A steady diet of pornography seems to numb them to the seriousness of sex crimes.

As the types of media expand, so do the possibilities for males—especially boys—to be exposed to images of violence against women. Cable television, available in most homes, is not subject to the same censorship as network television and shows more graphic sex and violence. Video games, played mainly by boys, are filled with violent scenes. And the Internet, which is now being used by many children both in school and at home, offers easy access to pornography.

Because these areas are relatively new, laws have not yet been created to regulate them. They are the subject of much debate by women's groups, parents, religious groups, free speech activists, Congress, and the courts.

The media in general have shown little sensitivity to women's concerns about their portrayal of sex roles and power. A country founded on freedom of speech and a free economy must also deal with the abuse of these freedoms by those who see financial gain in exploiting women.

5

Getting Help

ONE OF THE most important achievements of the women's movement in the 1970s was establishing a network of support services for abuse victims. Before shelters and counseling programs were created, battered women had nowhere to turn. Rape victims seldom reported their attacks, having no one to guide them through a legal system that favored their attackers. And treatment for violent men was almost unheard-of, so they continued their patterns of abuse.

For women in danger, the first step is finding a safe place to stay. The homes of friends or relatives are usually not the answer, since their abusers can easily track them there. For many women shelters are the best place to start to pick up the pieces of a shattered life. As one journalist notes, "Shelters were never meant to become permanent establishments, but because community institutions do not act effectively to defend women, shelters are the single most effective way of saving lives."[36]

Battered women's shelters

Temporary housing for battered women and their children exists throughout the country, although some areas have more shelters than others. Shelters are run by a variety of nonprofit organizations, including women's groups and churches. Their policies for limiting stays vary, and not all shelters are equipped to house children.

Local police departments, welfare departments, women's centers, hospitals, churches, therapists, and domestic violence hot lines are good sources for shelter referrals. In some states the police are required to provide victims of domestic violence with referrals to emergency housing, legal services, and counseling. Organizations such as the National Coalition Against Domestic Violence, which has a twenty-four-hour hot line, can also refer women to shelters nationwide.

Unfortunately, the shelter system is underfunded, and many shelters are forced to turn women away because of lack of space. Women sometimes must make several phone calls or travel a long distance to find a shelter that can take them, especially if they are bringing children. If all shelters in an area are full, they usually can refer women to other emergency housing.

Support and safety

Some women are reluctant to go to shelters, where they will be among strangers in a place that does not feel like a home. However, many come to see the experience as a positive one that helped them get on with their lives. One woman who stayed in a shelter until her abuser was jailed observes: "I didn't see anything good at first. Everyone had their own responsibilities. It was hard to adjust. . . . But eventually it was very healing for me. We sat and talked together and cried together."[37]

In addition to temporary housing and food, many shelters provide counseling and other services. Because many women are forced to flee their homes quickly, shelters often provide them with clothing and other necessities. They can arrange for emergency medical treatment for battered women and their children and help record their injuries for police and the courts. They can inform women of their legal rights, connect them with lawyers they can afford, and help them apply for financial aid and low-income housing.

The most important factor these shelters provide is safety from the abuser. The privacy of residents is protected and the location of the shelter is not made public. If an abuser finds the shelter where his partner is staying, the staff will only allow him in with the woman's consent. If

Battered women can start to rebuild their lives in the safety of a shelter. Most shelters provide temporary housing and meals, and some also offer counseling programs and help women obtain medical treatment, legal assistance, and permanent housing.

he locates the shelter by phone, the staff will take messages but not connect him to his victim. When husbands insist on seeing their children and their wives agree, many shelters can arrange a meeting in a controlled environment where the children cannot be harmed or kidnapped.

The average stay at a women's shelter is one to six weeks. Many women return to shelters three or four times before making a final break from their abusive partner.

Women who have a safe place to stay or are not ready to leave home can benefit from the outreach services some shelters offer. Many shelters have walk-in counseling programs in addition to counseling for residents.

Counseling for abused women

Counseling is an important step in recovering from domestic violence. It helps women stop blaming themselves for what has happened and take control of their lives.

Women who leave abusive relationships often feel guilty about abandoning their partners, particularly if children are involved. Counseling can help them understand that they are not responsible for their partner's behavior and need to focus on their own, and their children's, healing. A woman who suffered years of battering before fleeing with her children notes, "It didn't happen in a week, but they gave me my self-esteem back. He took my pride, my self-esteem, my energy and my strength. He took my friends and my family. He took everything. It took me a long time to even trust my counselor because he took all that away from me."[38]

Counselors at shelters help battered women set goals, such as getting a divorce, developing job skills, and finding employment. Many shelters and family crisis centers have long-term support groups that help women understand their situation, express their feelings, and regain their self-esteem. These groups provide women with the support of others in the same situation. This support can help battered women who have been isolated by their partners to realize that they are not alone with their problems and to reconnect with the outside world. Many shelter counselors are formerly battered women, who serve as role models for those seeking to escape domestic violence.

An important part of counseling is helping women survive on their own economically. A lack of financial resources is the main reason many women stay with abusive partners. When they finally leave, they need help in becoming self-supporting.

Help in becoming financially independent

Many abused women are pressured into total financial dependence on their partners. Batterers often force their wives to quit their jobs to devote themselves completely to their husbands. These men tend to take control of all the family's finances, putting all property, bank accounts, insurance, and credit cards in their own names. This is calculated to make it almost impossible for their partners to exist on their own. Many battered women are financial prisoners of their abusers.

Some shelters and women's organizations offer financial counseling or can make referrals to counseling and job training services. They can help women establish credit, get loans, or apply for public assistance until they find employment. Attorneys, many of whom provide free services to women in financial need, can help abused women get a fair share of their husband's assets. When these women file for divorce, the attorneys can assist them with property settlements and child support. It is recommended that battered women find divorce lawyers who have experience with domestic violence cases.

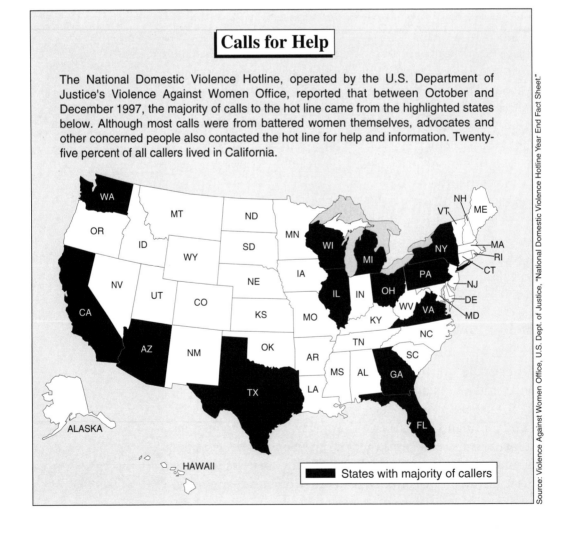

Calls for Help

The National Domestic Violence Hotline, operated by the U.S. Department of Justice's Violence Against Women Office, reported that between October and December 1997, the majority of calls to the hot line came from the highlighted states below. Although most calls were from battered women themselves, advocates and other concerned people also contacted the hot line for help and information. Twenty-five percent of all callers lived in California.

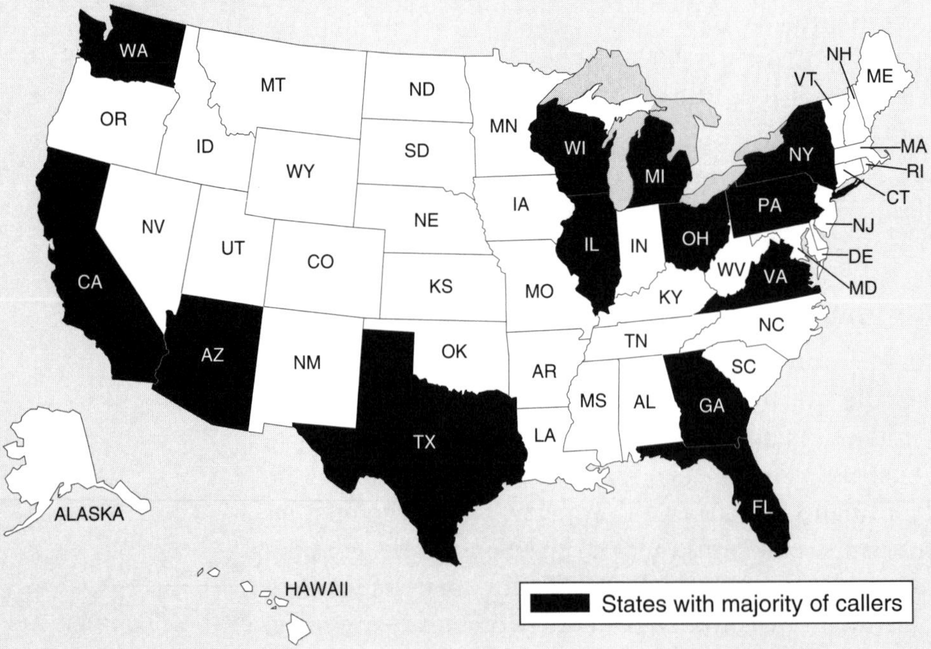

Source: Violence Against Women Office, U.S. Dept. of Justice, "National Domestic Violence Hotline Year End Fact Sheet."

Treatment for abusive partners

There is little agreement on how effective programs are in treating abusive men. One problem is that most men who enter treatment do so under court order; thus, they are being forced into therapy rather than choosing it. Those who attend by choice often do so only to keep their partners from leaving them or to get them back, and they often drop out once the women agree to stay. However, few men receive long jail sentences for beating their partners, and most will repeat their abusive behavior if they do not receive treatment.

Counselors also disagree about which type of treatment works best on batterers. Some see battering as a product of a sexist society and seek to change men's attitudes toward women. A counselor at the Boston treatment center EMERGE notes, "What's at the core of this problem is that men don't respect women. What needs to change is that sense of entitlement—that it is their right to control the lives of their partners. Battering is not a sickness, it's a learned behavior."[39]

Others, however, believe violence results from traumatic childhood experiences and treat it as a psychological problem. A counselor at the Center for Non-Violence in New Bedford, Massachusetts, takes this approach, stating that "if you want to make the effects of treatment last, you've got to make these men change from the inside out. If all you do is threaten them with the court and jail, it won't last. We try to help them understand why and when they're violent."[40]

Prevention programs for batterers began in the mid-1970s, and today there are about two hundred programs throughout the United States. Most men are treated in groups, and their reported success rates vary widely. A 1993 study shows that 35 percent of treated batterers repeated their behavior six months or more after treatment, as opposed to 52 percent of those who failed to complete their program. However, police reports show repeat offense rates three times higher for men who fail to receive treatment. A ten-year follow-up study of treated and untreated men shows that the latter are arrested twice as often. Those most likely to repeat their abuse are young, have problems with alcohol abuse, and have a longer history of violence than those who stop.

Court-ordered vs. voluntary programs

Court-ordered programs seem to be more successful than voluntary ones because the abusers are jailed (or receive longer sentences) if they do not complete them. Even with the threat of jail time, completion rates of those studied are 50 percent or less. These programs can vary in length from three months to seven or more, and the longer programs have poorer completion rates.

Most men who commit domestic violence are difficult to treat. They tend to deny their behavior or to blame it on others, and they are seldom motivated to change. Some have serious personality disorders that do not respond well to group therapy, where they are encouraged to face their shame in front of others.

In batterers' groups, negative views of women are challenged. Men are forced to accept responsibility for their actions. They are taught to recognize the feelings beneath their anger and to express themselves in ways other than violence, such as through negotiation and compromise. As they get to know one another, they confront members who are not being honest about their problems.

A batterer whose jail sentence included a court-ordered treatment program says, "When I first got into the program, I didn't know what to expect. I couldn't imagine sharing my problems with a bunch of strangers. But this is something I needed for myself and my kids." Describing the program's philosophy, he says, "They continually stressed that it was our behavior that got us in this situation. It's not what she did or what she said—we had to take responsibility for our actions."[41]

Studies show that although many men continue to abuse their partners after treatment, the number of attacks is greatly reduced. Some men who complete their treatment go into long-term support groups or twelve-step programs similar to those of Alcoholics Anonymous, which reduce their chances of returning to violence. Some become group facilitators, using their own recovery to help others.

While few people argue against trying to help men overcome their abusive behavior, women's groups strongly object to the courts using treatment as an alternative to jail sentences. They feel that unless men are punished for their crimes, they will not see domestic violence as a serious offense. Jailing offenders is also the only way their partners are guaranteed a chance to restart their lives without fear of another attack. Most advocates for battered women argue for a combination of jail time and required treatment.

Help for rape victims

Rape victims need medical attention as well as counseling and legal support. Many victims are severely injured in their attack, and they need to be concerned about sexually transmitted diseases, particularly AIDS, and the possibility of pregnancy. Most hospital emergency rooms are now trained to deal with the special needs of rape victims.

Counseling is an important step in recovering from rape. During counseling sessions women can work through the trauma they experienced and learn new ways to cope with fears associated with the rape.

Women who have been raped need counseling to overcome feelings of guilt, shame, and fear. They may feel that they are somehow responsible for what happened even when they know it is not rational. They often have trouble dealing with a partner's reaction to the attack, and many partners of rape victims need counseling as well. They may blame the woman for provoking the attack or themselves for not being there to protect her. Women who have been raped may also be afraid of any sexual contact, which puts a further strain on their relationships.

Some rape victims are in a state of shock after the attack and may bury their memories of it to protect themselves from reliving the pain. Without counseling they may develop post-traumatic stress disorder, which includes feelings of fear, anger, guilt, and depression that can show up months or even years after the attack. Experienced rape counselors understand this and encourage women to work through their feelings instead of denying them.

Many hospitals that treat rape victims provide counseling services or refer women to qualified counselors. Social service organizations, women's groups, and shelters can also make referrals.

There are more resources today than ever before to help victims of all types of abuse. There is also increased recognition that abusers need help as well to stop the cycle of violence. However, some critics feel that these programs do not do enough to actually end domestic violence. They argue for more education and early intervention to stop men from expressing their feelings through violence.

6

Looking Toward the Future: Proposals for Change

ENORMOUS ADVANCES HAVE been made over the last two decades in the treatment of abused women and the prosecution of their abusers. Women's accusations are taken much more seriously, and they are much less likely to be blamed for inviting their assaults. Police departments are quicker to respond to domestic violence complaints and to treat partner abuse as a serious crime. Date rapists, who once got away with their behavior, are being prosecuted far more often, and the "she asked for it" defense is failing to work for them.

Despite all these improvements, large numbers of women continue to be beaten, stalked, and raped. Many women feel that the social service and criminal justice systems are not doing enough to prevent violence against them. They believe that the police, courts, and agencies designed to protect women are often at cross purposes instead of coordinating their efforts.

There have been many proposals to change the ways government agencies approach male-on-female crime. Some involve changing the ways these agencies work together, while others focus on enacting tough new laws with high penalties for violent behavior. One area where changes are recommended is the way police departments deal with domestic violence cases.

Improving police response

Some police departments have excellent records of responding to domestic violence calls and programs for dealing with this type of crime. However, department rules vary from state to state and sometimes between cities, so women in different parts of the country do not have equal protection. Many advocates for battered women believe that police in all states should be required to arrest men without warrants if there is probable cause and hold them in jail overnight until their hearing before a judge.

Another proposal is to have all police departments computerize records of domestic violence calls. This allows officers to check an offender's history each time they receive a call, and they can easily identify repeat offenders who pose serious risk to their partners. Computerized records of restraining orders can also help police arrest men who violate them. Once all departments have a computerized system, they could be linked nationwide to track violators who move between states.

A further suggestion is that all police be required to provide abused women with printed information on their legal rights and the community services available to them. Women in a crisis situation often do not know where to

A 911 operator responds to emergency calls. Battered women's advocates propose that police departments establish a national computerized database to track domestic violence–related calls.

turn for help. This information should be offered in privacy so that the abusive partner cannot track down a woman who flees to safety. Officers could also be required in all states to offer to bring victims to a safe place where their attackers, when released, cannot reach them.

Massachusetts is one of the leading states in providing police protection for battered women, and its program could be used as a model for states that need stronger approaches. In addition to mandatory arrest of offenders, Massachusetts police officers are directed to remove firearms from the home and keep a registry of restraining orders to spot violators. They coordinate their efforts with local educators and victim advocates and participate in the state's Violence Prevention Program, in which officers help students learn nonviolent behavior in relationships.

Education

Those concerned with violence against women feel that education is key to its prevention. This includes educating children about healthy and unhealthy relationships, as well as teaching adults to recognize the signs of abusive behavior and respond to them before they cause serious harm.

The Violence Prevention Program in Massachusetts is a strong model for teaching children about domestic violence and its prevention. It is also a good example of how several agencies can work together toward violence prevention. The program was designed by staff members of a shelter for battered women. Working with seventh- and eighth-grade students, male-female teams consisting of one police officer and one teacher model respectful behavior between the sexes. In five one-hour sessions, the teams role-play and lead students in discussions of how men and women should resolve their conflicts and treat one another. They explain stereotyping—labeling an entire group of people, such as women, as being a certain way—and explore it through advertisements, showing how it creates an imbalance of power between the sexes. They often invite former batterers and victims to speak in an effort to expose some of the myths about battering.

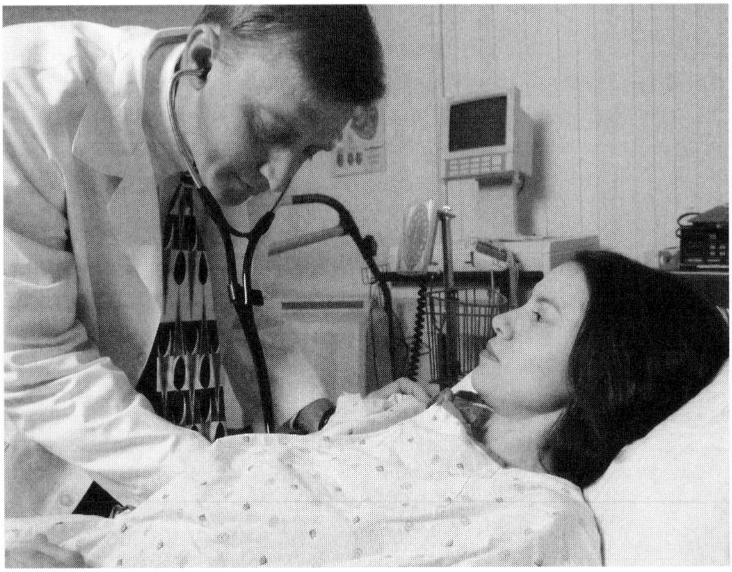

Since battered women are often forced to seek medical treatment for their injuries, many health care professionals believe that doctors should be trained to recognize the signs of domestic violence and intervene to prevent its reoccurrence.

Students who evaluated the program felt that it would be helpful in preventing violence in their relationships. A survey of these students showed an improved ability to identify abusive behavior.

Another area where domestic violence education is increasing is in the medical community. Hospitals and medical and nursing associations are recognizing that they play an important role in helping injured women and preventing their future abuse.

Involving the medical community

Hospital emergency rooms or doctor's offices are often the first places where cases of domestic violence are recognized. Battered women can often hide their bruises from friends and coworkers, but they are evident on the examining table. Since over half of battered women suffer injuries and at least one-quarter seek medical treatment, doctors need to be alert to the signs of domestic violence and urge women to get help.

One survey estimates that doctors recognize only one out of twenty-five cases of battering in their patients, and fewer than half of medical schools in the United States provide special training on dealing with domestic assault.

According to a 1991 study of health professionals, "Family violence is recognized as a major problem at the health care systems level" but "little and inadequate attention is given to prevention, identification, treatment and follow-up of cases."[42]

In 1991 the American Medical Association announced its campaign against family violence. Its director recommended that medical personnel be required to report domestic violence to the police, but the AMA issued guidelines rather than requirements. Some experts believe that forcing doctors to report abuse could backfire by putting victims at increased risk from their partners. Instead, they recommend that doctors put patients in touch with community resources that can help them, such as family crisis centers and battered women's shelters.

Educating health care professionals

The American Nurses Association has become involved in educating nurses and other health care providers in domestic violence prevention. In a position statement, the ANA asserts that "there is a need to increase awareness to the health problem of violence against women, as well as reduce injuries and psychological misery associated with this crime. ANA believes health care professionals must be educated as to their role in the assessment, intervention and prevention of physical violence against women."[43] The ANA recommends paying special attention to women who are at increased risk of abuse, such as pregnant women, as well as educating all women about the cycle of violence and teaching children about violent relationships.

Advocates for battered women recommend that all emergency rooms have a professional on staff or on call from a battered women's program to evaluate cases of partner and child abuse and help women plan for their safety. They note that women must be able to bring their children in for medical care without worrying that they will be accused of child abuse. Children's Hospital in Boston runs a model program, Advocacy for Women and Kids in Emergencies (AWAKE), for working with battered women and their children. It offers counseling, help in finding emergency shelter, referrals for legal help, and support groups. The program also trains health care professionals to identify and treat victims of domestic violence and helps other organizations set up similar programs.

Medical staff need to be able to refer women to lawyers who can help them break free of their abusive partners. This means that lawyers must also have special training in dealing with domestic abuse.

Progress in the courts

Women who take the risk of leaving their abusers need to know that the legal system will help them remain safe. Some states have set up programs that provide special training for court workers in handling domestic abuse cases.

The Pace University Battered Women's Justice Center in New York was the first university-based center in the United States to train lawyers to represent battered women. Established in 1991, the center teaches prosecutors to provide better legal representation, promotes free legal services to battered women, works toward creating new laws to stop violence, and does legal research and publishes ar-

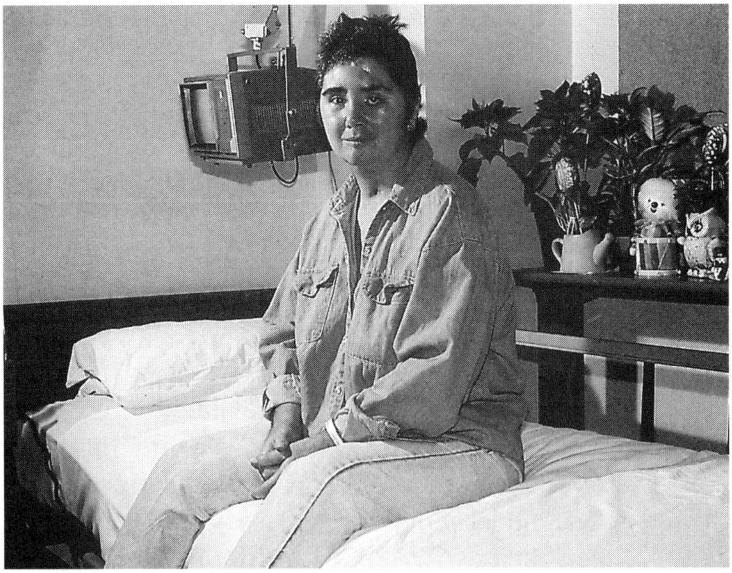

A battered woman sits in a hospital room after her boyfriend fractured her skull with a baseball bat when she tried to break up with him.

ticles on domestic violence. Its director asserts: "We must accept that the justice system has not effectively protected women from abuse. Our legal system is only now beginning to understand that these cases are probably more serious than 'stranger assault' because the potential for escalating violence is much greater."[44]

The Pace program, with its focus on education, could serve as a model for others throughout the country. Another successful program that could be adapted by other cities is the Domestic Abuse Intervention Project in Duluth, Minnesota. Established in 1980, this project links police officers, prosecutors, civil and criminal court judges, and probation officers in its effort to help battered women through the court system.

Women's advocates

Many people believe that paid women's advocates should be in every prosecutor's office and court to advise battered women of their rights and guide them through the legal system. They recommend that the courts set up support and education groups for battered women. Other suggestions include making it easier to get restraining orders, including on weekends, having computerized records of these orders in the courts, and sending violators of these orders to jail.

Battered women's advocates have also been fighting to let civil court judges review the criminal records of offenders and consider them in sentencing. They have been demanding heavier sentences for repeat offenders, and they want judges in all states to have the power to remove batterers from the home and order them to stay away. Advocates recommend that sentences include treatment for offenders but that treatment programs never replace jail time.

The law is the area that has seen the most progress in fighting violence against women. Women's groups targeted the law in the 1970s and have continued over the years to press for tougher, more effective measures to protect victims and punish their abusers. This has led to many changes in the law and to new legislation, such as the creation of antistalking laws throughout the nation. However, many prosecutors and others who fight for victims' rights feel that the law still has a long way to go.

The Violence Against Women Act

Because most laws covering rape and abuse are written by individual states, there is great variation in how much protection women have in different parts of the country. The Violence Against Women Act (VAWA) was signed into law by President Clinton in 1994 to help victims of assault nationwide. One of its goals is to protect battered women who cross state lines. Protection orders from one state must now be recognized in all others, and abusers who follow their victim into another state face strong penalties for violating their order. The act helps federal, state, and local prosecutors work together to determine who can best prosecute a case. It also includes a ban on gun possession by domestic abusers.

A mother and daughter participate in a rally against domestic violence. The Violence Against Women Act has increased public awareness and strengthened prevention programs nationwide.

Under VAWA, federal funding to the states for programs to stop domestic violence increased. In 1995 the Department of Justice S*T*O*P Violence Against Women grant program (Services*Training*Officers*Prosecutors) provided $26 million to states and Indian tribes to help them respond to violent crimes against women; in 1996 the amount was increased to $130 million, and Congress approved another $28 million for grants to another program, Encourage Arrest Policies. In the same year, the Department of Justice awarded $46 million under the Community Oriented Policing to Combat Domestic Violence grant program.

The attention domestic violence is receiving from the federal government is helping efforts by states across the country. The federal attorney general's office notes, "This

Administration and the Attorney General are committed to the tough enforcement of the VAWA criminal provisions. By working in partnership with our state and local counterparts, we can stop batterers from slipping through the cracks of the criminal justice system as easily as they cross state lines."[45]

State laws

Some of the toughest new laws have been enacted by states. In Arizona, some rapists and other sex offenders are released into lifetime probation after serving their jail time. They must pass regular lie detector tests about their behavior and attend individual and group therapy. In addition, officers assigned to watch them can enter their homes unannounced at any time. The U.S. Supreme Court recently ruled that other states have the right to set up similar programs. One reporter states, "The premise of the Arizona law is that sex offenders cannot be rehabilitated; they can merely be prevented from acting again. The National Institute of Justice, the research arm of the U.S. Department of Justice, declared earlier this year that 'A "cure" for sex offending is no more available than a cure for epilepsy or high blood pressure.' "[46] While many critics argue that such laws are too harsh, others point to their effectiveness. A three-year study of eleven hundred men under this program in Maricopa County, Arizona, shows that only 1.5 percent repeated their crimes.

The recent popularity of tough sentencing for sex offenders has prompted some politicians to include them in their push for broadening the death penalty. Al Checchi, a candidate for governor of California, recently ran campaign ads calling for the death penalty for serial rapists and child molesters, saying, "Killing the spirit of a woman or a child is and should be a capital offense."[47] Such laws are unlikely to be passed, however. In 1977 the U.S. Supreme Court ruled that extending the death penalty to rape cases was unconstitutional, and death penalty laws for rapists were overturned in Tennessee, Florida, and Mississippi.

Prosecutors and others who fight for victims' rights recognize that the law has come a long way in making crime against women a serious issue. Penalties for abuse have increased, and a national effort has strengthened the work of individual cities and states.

All these advances are intended to encourage women to report their abuse and break away from their abusers. Some people argue that this is only giving women false hope since there are still not enough places for them to turn for their most basic need: a home away from the one they left behind.

Expanding the shelter system

Until domestic violence can be reduced, more safe places are needed to house its victims. The battered women's shelter system does not meet current needs. There are too few shelters, and those that exist lack funds for programs and trained staffing. Many have been forced to fire paid workers and cut back on services, such as programs for children.

The director of the Pace University Battered Women's Justice Center describes the problem in New York: "In New York last year we were able to house about 12,000 battered women and children, but we turned away about 25,000 more because of lack of space. We still live in a country that has three times as many animal shelters as battered women's shelters."[48]

While much of their focus has been on stopping violence, advocates for battered women recognize that it will not go away overnight. By encouraging more women to leave their abusive homes, they are flooding a system that was not built to handle so many people in need. They are pressuring government and private groups to provide funding to build more safe houses that can accept women with their children, set up programs that meet more of their needs, and train and pay staff so that shelters do not have to depend on volunteers.

There is also the hard truth that shelters are only temporary homes, and many battered women lack the resources to move into market-rate housing. More programs are needed to find long-term solutions for women with limited money and credit. Shelters could be linked with programs that move poor women and their children into affordable housing.

A great deal of progress has been made over the last twenty years in advancing women's rights and bringing the problems of violence against women out of the shadows. Public awareness of domestic violence, rape, and other forms of abuse has helped change the laws to provide better protection for women against men who abuse their power. However, two decades of change are not enough to undo centuries of damage, and the fight to change many men's attitudes toward women continues in the courts, in the press, and in organizations throughout the country.

These proposals for change are encouraging signs that violence against women is being taken seriously in the United States. There is greater awareness of the problem than ever before and more debate on the best ways to deal with its consequences when prevention fails. Domestic violence, rape, stalking, and other threats to women's safety are now issues in the public eye and promise to remain so until women are truly safe from abuse.

Notes

Chapter 1: Domestic Violence and the Law

1. Quoted in Alison B. Landes, Suzanne Squyres, and Jacqueline Quiram, eds., *Violent Relationships: Battering and Abuse Among Adults*. Wylie, TX: Information Plus, 1997, p. 10.

2. Quoted in Landes, Squyres, and Quiram, *Violent Relationships*, pp. 2–3.

3. Quoted in Landes, Squyres, and Quiram, *Violent Relationships*, p. 4.

4. Quoted in Ann Jones, *Next Time, She'll Be Dead: Battering and How to Stop It*. Boston: Beacon Press, 1994, p. 52.

5. Quoted in Jones, *Next Time, She'll Be Dead*, p. 63.

6. Quoted in Jones, *Next Time, She'll Be Dead*, p. 64.

7. Quoted in Landes, Squyres, and Quiram, *Violent Relationships*, p. 91.

8. Quoted in Landes, Squyres, and Quiram, *Violent Relationships*, p. 89.

Chapter 2: The Nature of Domestic Violence

9. Theresa M. Zubretsky, "Adult Domestic Violence: The Alcohol Connection," October 9, 1995. On-line. Internet. Available http://www.serve.com/zone/alcohol/keynote.html.

10. Quoted in Susan Murphy-Milano, *Defending Our Lives: Getting Away from Domestic Violence and Staying Safe*. New York: Doubleday, 1996, p. 41.

11. Quoted in Jones, *Next Time, She'll Be Dead*, p. 184.

12. Quoted in Landes, Squyres, and Quiram, *Violent Relationships*, p. 43.

13. Quoted in Landes, Squyres, and Quiram, *Violent Relationships*, p. 26.

14. Quoted in Jones, *Next Time, She'll Be Dead*, p. 32.

15. Quoted in Jones, *Next Time, She'll Be Dead*, p. 185.

Chapter 3: Rape

16. Quoted in Robin Warshaw, *I Never Called It Rape: The* Ms. *Report on Recognizing, Fighting, and Surviving Date and Acquaintance Rape*. New York: Harper & Row, 1988, p. 23.

17. Quoted in Warshaw, *I Never Called It Rape*, p. 39.

18. Quoted in Warshaw, *I Never Called It Rape*, p. 39.

19. Katie Roiphe, "Date Rape's Other Victim," *New York Times Magazine*, June 13, 1993. On-line. Internet. Available http://www.vix.com/pub/men/books/roiphe.html.

20. Quoted in Roiphe, "Date Rape's Other Victim."

21. Roiphe, "Date Rape's Other Victim."

22. Roiphe, "Date Rape's Other Victim."

23. Quoted in Landes, Squyres, and Quiram, *Violent Relationships*, p. 54.

24. Linda Fairstein, *Sexual Violence: Our War Against Rape*. New York: Morrow, 1993, p. 15.

25. Fairstein, *Sexual Violence*, p. 81.

26. Fairstein, *Sexual Violence*, p. 41.

Chapter 4: Sex and Violence in American Culture

27. Quoted in Robert Lovinger, "Culture Shock: Too Much Violence? Some Critics Suggest Accumulation of Mayhem Can Make a Difference," *Standard-Times*, n.d. On-line. Internet. Available http://www.s-t.com/projects/DomVio/cultureshock.html.

28. Quoted in Carol Wekesser, ed., *Pornography: Opposing Viewpoints*. San Diego: Greenhaven Press, 1997, pp. 22–23.

29. Quoted in Lovinger, "Culture Shock."

30. Quoted in Mary E. Williams and Tamara L. Roleff, eds.,

Sexual Violence: Opposing Viewpoints. San Diego: Greenhaven Press, 1997, p. 32.

31. Quoted in Williams and Roleff, eds., *Sexual Violence*, p. 34.

32. Quoted in Wekesser, ed., *Pornography*, p. 26.

33. Quoted in Wekesser, ed., *Pornography*, p. 25.

34. Quoted in Williams and Roleff, eds., *Sexual Violence,* p. 19.

35. Quoted in Marjorie Heins, *Sex, Sin, and Blasphemy: A Guide to America's Censorship Wars*. New York: Free Press, 1993, p. 159.

Chapter 5: Getting Help

36. Jones, *Next Time, She'll Be Dead*, p. 230.

37. Quoted in Patricia O'Connor, "Frightened Women Rebuild Their Lives," *Standard-Times*, n.d. On-line. Internet. Available http://www.s-t.com/projects/DomVio/frightenedwomen.html.

38. Quoted in O'Connor, "Frightened Women Rebuild Their Lives."

39. Quoted in Bill Ibelle, "Debate Rages on Batterers' Treatment: Can Abusers Be Cured, or Must They Be Punished?" *Standard-Times*, n.d. On-line. Internet. Available http://www.s-t.com/projects/DomVio/debatetreatment.html.

40. Quoted in Ibelle, "Debate Rages on Batterers' Treatment."

41. Quoted in Ibelle, "Why Batterers Do What They Do: Donald Says the Day of His Arrest Was the Luckiest Day of His Life," *Standard-Times*, n.d. On-line. Internet. Available http://www.s-t.com/projects/DomVio/luckyday.html.

Chapter 6: Looking Toward the Future: Proposals for Change

42. Quoted in Jones, *Next Time, She'll Be Dead*, p. 148.

43. American Nurses Association, position statement, "Physical Violence Against Women," n.d. On-line. Internet. Available http://www.ana.org/readroom/ position/social/scviol.htm.

44. Battered Women's Justice Center, brochure, May 20, 1996. On-line. Internet. Available http://orion.law.pace.edu/bwjc/brochur1.htm.

45. U.S. Department of Justice, *Violence Against Women Act News*, vol. 1, July 1996. On-line. Internet. Available http://www.usdoj.gov/vawo/newsletter/js796.htm.

46. Mike Tharp, "Tracking Sexual Impulses: An Intrusive Program to Stop Offenders from Striking Again." *U.S. News & World Report*, July 7, 1997. On-line. Internet. Available http://www.usnews.com/usnews/issue/970707/7sex.htm.

47. Quoted in Robert B. Gunnison, "Al Checchi Goes Out on a Limb: Upping the Ante, the Candidate for Governor Wants the Death Penalty to Be Extended to Serial Rapists and Repeat Child Molesters," *San Francisco Chronicle*, February 8, 1998, p. 3.

48. Battered Women's Justice Center, brochure.

Organizations to Contact

EMERGE: Counseling and Education to Stop Male Violence
2380 Massachusetts Ave.
Cambridge, MA 02140
(617) 422-1550

This organization offers group counseling for men who have abused women, training courses on working with abusive men, provides public speakers on domestic violence, and offers referrals to services for battered women.

National Clearinghouse on Marital and Date Rape
web address: http://members.aol.com/ncmdr/index.html

This organization conducts research and public speaking on issues of marital and date rape. It invites visitors to its website to print materials and offers links to other related sites.

National Coalition Against Domestic Violence (NCADV)
(303) 839-1852 or (800) 799-7233

The NCADV provides information and referrals for abused women and their children. It runs a twenty-four-hour hot line for victims of domestic violence.

National Domestic Violence Hotline
(800) 799-SAFE (7233)

This government-sponsored hot line assists domestic violence victims and fields about eight thousand calls a month. It is linked to a database containing information about battered women's shelters, legal assistance programs, and social service programs throughout the United States.

Suggestions for Further Reading

Susan Brewster, *To Be an Anchor in the Storm: A Guide for Families and Friends of Abused Women.* New York: Ballantine Books, 1997. This guide is for people who want to help a friend or loved one in her struggle to escape domestic violence. The author, a survivor of battering, has counseled abused women for over ten years and uses lessons from her own life along with case histories. She discusses how to recognize the signs of abuse, become a better advocate for battered women, and deal with batterers.

Rus Ervin Funk, *Stopping Rape: A Challenge for Men.* Philadelphia: New Society, 1993. This book provides insights and exercises to help men end their violence against women and assist others. The author uses stories and "action steps" to help men understand how rape affects women and organize to stop sexual abuse.

Joyce Johnson, *What Lisa Knew: The Truth and Lies About the Steinberg Case.* New York: Putnam, 1990. The author examines the murder case against Joel Steinberg, whose brutal abuse of his partner, Hedda Nussbaum, and their illegally adopted daughter, Lisa, brought national attention to the horrors of domestic violence.

Esther Madriz, *Nothing Bad Happens to Good Girls: Fear of Crime in Women's Lives.* Berkeley: University of California Press, 1997. This book explores women's fear of violent crime. Through interviews, the author shows how the threat of violence increases the inequalities between the sexes and contributes to the social control of women by men.

Darcy O'Brien, *Power to Hurt: Inside a Judge's Chambers: Sexual Assault, Corruption, and the Ultimate Reversal of Justice for Women*. New York: HarperCollins, 1996. The author relates the story of how eight women were abused by a judge, including through stalking and rape, and found the courage to stand up against him in court. The judge was sentenced to twenty-five years in prison for violating their civil rights.

Sheila Weller, *Saint of Circumstance: The Untold Story Behind the Alex Kelly Rape Case: Growing Up Rich and Out of Control*. New York: Pocket Books, 1998. This book relates the events leading to the conviction of serial acquaintance rapist Alex Kelly. Kelly, age fifteen at the time of his first reported sexual assault, escaped justice abroad for eight years with the help of his parents.

Works Consulted

American Bar Association Commission on Domestic Violence, "Multidisciplinary Responses to Domestic Violence," n.d. On-line. Internet. Available http://www.abanet.org/domviol/mrdv/facts.html.

American Nurses Association, position statement, "Physical Violence Against Women," n.d. On-line. Internet. Available http://www.ana.org/readroom/position/social/scviol.htm.

Associated Press, "Violence Study Spurs Call to Arms," *Deseret News*, n.d. On-line. Internet. Available http://www.desnews.com/cyber/bytes/byte0207.htm.

William D. Baker, "September 1995 Police Practice Prevention: A New Approach to Domestic Violence," n.d. On-line. Internet. Available http://www.ici.net/cust_pages/jdemtd/domestic.htm.

Battered Women's Justice Center, brochure, May 20, 1996. On-line. Internet. Available http://orion.law.pace.edu/bwjc/brochur1.htm.

Linda Fairstein, *Sexual Violence: Our War Against Rape*. New York: Morrow, 1993.

Robert B. Gunnison, "Al Checchi Goes Out on a Limb: Upping the Ante, the Candidate for Governor Wants the Death Penalty to Be Extended to Serial Rapists and Repeat Child Molestors," *San Francisco Chronicle*, February 8, 1998.

Marjorie Heins, *Sex, Sin, and Blasphemy: A Guide to America's Censorship Wars*. New York: Free Press, 1993.

Ann Jones, *Next Time, She'll Be Dead: Battering and How to Stop It*. Boston: Beacon Press, 1994.

J. Kahn, "Domestic Violence Laws May Do More Harm Than Good," *Medical Tribune*, July 13, 1995. On-line. Internet. Available http://www.thriveonline.com@@Ddp VwgQAiluiiErc/thrive/health/Library/CAD/abstract23234.11 /9/98.

Alison B. Landes, Suzanne Squyres, and Jacqueline Quiram, eds., *Violent Relationships: Battering and Abuse Among Adults*. Wylie, TX: Information Plus, 1997.

Susan Murphy-Milano, *Defending Our Lives: Getting Away from Domestic Violence and Staying Safe*. New York: Doubleday, 1996.

Katie Roiphe, "Date Rape's Other Victim," *New York Times Magazine*, June 13, 1993. On-line. Internet. Available http://www.vix.com/pub/men/books/roiphe.html.

Joan Silverstein, "Prosecutions Under the Violence Against Women Act," *Violence Against Women Act News*, vol. 1, July 1996. On-line. Internet. Available http://www.usdoj.gov/vawo/newsletter/js796.htm.

Jan Berliner Slatman, *The Battered Woman's Survival Guide: Breaking the Cycle*. Dallas: Taylor, 1990.

Standard-Times, series of sixty articles on domestic violence. On-line. Internet. Available http://www.s-t.com/projects/DomVio/.

Donald G. Sutton, with Susan K. Golant, *The Batterer: A Psychological Profile*. New York: BasicBooks, 1995.

Mike Tharp, "Tracking Sexual Impulses: An Intrusive Program to Stop Offenders from Striking Again," *U.S. News & World Report*, July 7, 1997. On-line. Internet. Available http://www.usnews.com/usnews/issue/970707/7sex.htm.

U.S. Department of Justice, "Violence Against Women Act Fact Sheet," August 7, 1996. On-line. Internet. Available http://www.usdoj.gov/vawo/vawafct.htm.

Robin Warshaw, *I Never Called It Rape: The* Ms. *Report on Recognizing, Fighting, and Surviving Date and Acquaintance Rape*. New York: Harper & Row, 1988.

Carol Wekesser, ed., *Pornography: Opposing Viewpoints*. San Diego: Greenhaven Press, 1997.

Mary E. Williams and Tamara L. Roleff, eds., *Sexual Violence: Opposing Viewpoints*. San Diego: Greenhaven Press, 1997.

Theresa M. Zubretsky, "Adult Domestic Violence: The Alcohol Connection," October 9, 1995. On-line. Internet. Available http://www.serve.com/zone/alcohol/keynote.html.

Index

Picture Credits

Cover photo: © Viviane Moss/Saba
© Ed Braverman/FPG International, 27
© Ron Chapple/FPG International, 41, 43
© 1990 Robert Fox/Impact Visuals, 51
Natasha Frost, 35, 64
© Jeff Greenberg/Archive Photos, 53
© Ansell Horn/Impact Visuals, 76
© Marilyn Humphries/Impact Visuals, 17
© Robert Maass/Sipa Press, 47, 69
© 1992 Ken Martin/Impact Visuals, 15
© Tom McKitterick/Impact Visuals, 38
© Crady von Pawlak/Archive Photos, 49
PhotoDisc, 31, 72, 74
© Rickerby/Sipa Press, 56
© 1997 Shia Photo/Impact Visuals, 7
© Mark Scott/FPG International, 23
UPI/Corbis-Bettmann, 11, 29

About the Author

Lisa Wolff is a writer and editor with many years of staff experience at New York publishing houses. She currently lives in San Diego, where she edits reference books and writes articles on health and books on social issues.